A BOOK FOR
FAMILY
READING

A BOOK FOR
FAMILY
READING

How to cook a crow
and other stories that teach biblical truth

Jim Cromarty

 EVANGELICAL PRESS

EVANGELICAL PRESS
12 Wooler Street, Darlington, Co. Durham, DL1 1RQ, England

© Evangelical Press 1995
First published 1995

British Library Cataloguing in Publication Data available

ISBN 0 85234 339 6

Printed in Great Britain at The Bath Press, Avon

To my dear wife Valerie
without whose encouragement I would not have
written these stories which teach the great truths of
God's Word.

Contents

Foreword

This book comes from the heart and pen of a pastor and evangelist. Its central focus is the gospel, and the reader is constantly brought face to face with the claims of Christ.

Its author, Jim Cromarty, has a natural gift of telling entertaining stories, and here he directs that gift to presenting the gospel. He brings his long experience as a teacher and school principal to bear on applying biblical truths. He also knows well the needs from a pastoral situation, especially how biblical truth has to be explained and then directed to the heart and mind.

While I can identify with his writing, knowing well many of the areas in which the stories are based, yet I am sure that this book is going to appeal to a broad readership. The stories are dealing with human life in all its variety, and they are written in an easy and attractive style.

I commend it very warmly, and trust that this is only the first of his writings which many will read, and from them gain spiritual blessing.

Allan M. Harman
Presbyterian Theological College
Melbourne

Preface

The most wonderful thing that could happen to any person is that he or she come to faith in Christ. This book has been written to encourage you to turn from your sins and run to the Lord Jesus for salvation. The stories teach many of the great reformed truths that are found in the Bible.

We live in an age where our children are being fed a daily diet of violence and immorality through the various media. This means that Christian parents must provide their children with carefully selected meals of spiritual truth. Christian parents must closely supervise all the activities in which their children are involved and encourage them in the ways of righteousness. In this way we can help prepare them for life in the wider world.

Parents, generally, are willing to spend a fortune preparing their children for material success. Hours are spent encouraging them to do their best in the academic, sporting and entertainment world. Yet so few spend time teaching their children of the Creator and of their need of Christ, the Saviour of sinners. Jesus asked, 'What will it profit a man if he gains the whole world, and loses his soul?' (Mark 8:36). We must have our priorities correct and so teach our children the great truth found in the *Shorter Catechism*: 'Man's chief end is to glorify God and enjoy him for ever.'

What a tragedy it would be if our children gained much of the world and lost their soul! Death, judgement, hell and heaven are realities, as is the doctrine of election. We must tell our children God's truth in a way suitable to their age.

It is hoped that this series of stories will assist parents to do just that. After all, I am certain that when we lie down for the last time with the realization that death is near, the only thing that will matter is the saving love of Jesus Christ. Your faith in Christ will be your comfort. You will be able to look back on your life and know that only those things you did in the name of the Lord were really worthwhile.

I suggest that parents with young children read these stories with the Bible readings and, using the suggested activities as a guide, discuss the truths taught. Older children may read them alone, but should be encouraged to meditate upon the truths taught. The stories could also be of use for pastors and others, in presenting the gospel to young people — or even used as sermon illustrations.

I would urge all Christian parents to daily gather their family together and conduct family worship. The Word of God should be read and discussed. Prayer should be offered up to God. These stories could be the basis for some family worship times. There are fifty-two stories — maybe one for each Sunday over the forthcoming year.

It is my sincere prayer that God, through his Spirit, might use this small book to bring people to faith in Christ.

Activities

1. Spend time discussing the issues raised in each story. Several are provided at the conclusion of each chapter.
2. After each chapter has been studied, I suggest you encourage your child to memorize the text — as well as its place in the Bible.
3. Younger children could be encouraged to add some colour to the line drawings.

Remember

Be willing to sit down with your children and talk with them about spiritual issues. Always have an open ear to listen to their problems and their joys. Encourage your children by setting them an example of godly living. Uphold them before the Lord in your prayers.

Jim Cromarty

Cooking a crow

Read
Matthew 6:19-34

> 'But seek first the king-
> dom of God and His
> righteousness...'
> (Matthew 6:33).

I'm sure that when we come to the end of our lives and begin to look back over what has taken place, we shall say there were things we did that were a waste of time — they just weren't worth doing.

I'm sure that when we lay our heads down for the last time and realize that death is approaching, the only thing that will matter is the love of Jesus Christ. What a joy it will be on that day to know that our earthly pilgrimage is about to end, and that we are going to our eternal heavenly home to be with our Saviour! Our faith in Christ will be our true comfort. We shall look back on our lives and know that only those things we did in the Lord's name were really worthwhile.

When the British settlers landed on Australia's shores they had to learn to live off the land. When Governor Phillip landed with the many convicts they did not have much food with them. The new settlers would have had to dig gardens and plant crops. They would have had to catch animals for food. They would have had to catch fresh fish nearly every day. There were no refrigerators in Australia to keep food in, and I can well imagine that those settlers took careful notice of the native people and what they ate.

I'm sure that sometimes the settlers ate what they thought to be good bush foods, only to find out that they became sick, and in some cases died from the poisonous plants they ate. But there were plenty of birds, fish and land animals to eat.

There were plenty of crows in Australia and I believe that the early settlers tried cooking these birds. They had very tough flesh and an old bushman told me the way to cook a crow.

'Well,' he said, 'first you catch a crow and pluck out all of its feathers. Then you put a pot of water on the fire and bring the water to the boil. That is the easy part. Then you take a large stone and drop it in the pot. Carefully place the crow in the boiling water with the stone. All you have to do then is keep poking at the stone. When the stone is soft, throw the crow away and eat the stone.'

I'm sure that the man was pulling my leg. What he was really saying was, 'There are some things that are not worth doing, and one of them is to try to cook a crow to eat.'

The most important thing you can do in your life is to trust in the Lord Jesus Christ for your salvation. To spend your life serving Christ and glorifying God is the most wonderful thing in the world.

Our Bible passage reminds us that some people spend a lifetime making money, becoming a great sportsman, or just being a good family person, but these things will mean nothing when we face God on the Judgement Day. Of what use will be our lovely clothes, our nice home and big car on that day? Of what use will be all the worry and effort which we have put into getting the treasures of this world when we are called to stand before Christ's judgement-seat? All that will matter is our relationship with Jesus Christ.

Jesus said, 'For what will it profit a man if he gains the whole world, and loses his soul?' (Mark 8:36). There have been people in history who have tried to gain the world — or as much of it as possible. For a short time they have enjoyed themselves with their gains — but what happens to them in eternity after the judgement?

May each and every reader understand what Jesus is saying here. He is telling you that you can gain everything that the world has to offer — money, fame, honours, a good name, a wonderful home and a great big car; but if you die without Christ it will be an everlasting tragedy, for without Christ you will be cast into hell and eternally suffer the anger of God.

Activities

a. What are some of the things you have done that are a waste of time?
b. What is the most important thing in the world and why is it so important?

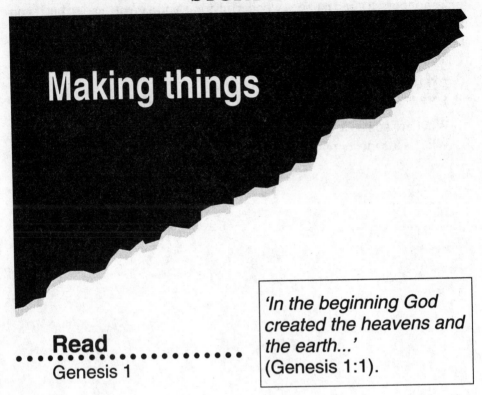

Making things

Read
Genesis 1

> 'In the beginning God created the heavens and the earth...'
> (Genesis 1:1).

I'm sure you all like making things. I'm not very good with a hammer and nail, but I like telling stories that teach. I also like tapestry, where I can weave colourful pictures using a needle and thread.

One of my grandsons, Scott, is a real maker of things. He has a box in which he keeps everything he can find. He has his own hammer and saw and is always using them to build something.

Whenever my wife and I have a box or something we think Scott might be able to use, we put it aside for him to collect. Then he puts it in his odds-and-ends box for future use. Sometimes when I visit his home, I can hear Scott hammering away in the garage. His father David has to check on him every now and again, because Scott likes to use his father's tools when he can and his father isn't very happy about it.

One day when we called in, we could hear Scott hammering away. I decided to find out what he was making. Scott wanted a cat as a pet, and even though his Dad had said, 'No,' Scott decided to try to win him over. So, there he was, building a home for the cat he hoped he would be allowed to get. The cat house had four or five rooms and the roof was made of clear plastic so he would be able to watch his pet all the time.

It took quite a long time to build the cat house, and when he had finished he proudly called his Mum and Dad to come out and look. Mum and Dad thought that Scott had done a great job, and his sister Jessica pleaded, 'Dad, can we get a cat now? We'll look after it.'

Dad was weakening and replied, 'We'll see.'

A week or so later the children had their new pets — two of them, one each. They were babies, but not what they had expected. They were baby rabbits. Scott and Jessica thought they were wonderful. The cat house was of no use for the rabbits and poor Dad had to build a hutch for them. It had to be well built for there were dogs about and the hutch needed to be strong enough to protect the baby rabbits.

We all see people making things and I'm sure you sometimes make something. But we use materials that we have. The Bible tells us that in the very beginning, God made the heavens and the earth, and everything found in them — out of *nothing*. God simply spoke the word and the heavens and earth came into existence. The Bible also tells us that God created the heavens and the earth, through his only Son, the Lord Jesus Christ. When we go out and look about us we can see God's wonderful creation. And what we see is truly glorious, even though sin has destroyed much of its beauty.

When I finish my tapestry, I have it framed so that people can look at it. Sometimes people comment that I have done a good job. One day my daughter Heather, who is an optometrist, pointed out that in one of my works I had missed a stitch in the eye of a lion. When God finished the work of creation in six days, he also looked at what he had done and declared that it 'was very good' (Genesis 1:31). Not one item had been omitted.

We are then told that God rested on the seventh day. God was not tired from working, but we have a picture of God looking at his creation and seeing how wonderful and perfect it was. The creation glorifies God, because in it we can see the power, the wisdom and the majesty of our God.

God created the light, the earth, the stars and the planets, the animals, the plants, the birds, the fish, the angels in heaven and man upon the earth. We are told that God created man in his own image. This means that man was created holy, and capable of friendship with God. Just as God is the great Ruler of the universe, so he gave man the job of ruling over the earth. Adam and Eve were capable of making good and God-honouring decisions. God gave the first man a special job to do, and that was to take care of the earth. God also made Adam a wife, Eve, out of his bone and flesh. Eve was a wonderful companion for Adam.

In those early days of creation, before there was any sin in the world, we are told that God walked in the Garden of Eden to talk with Adam and Eve. Everything was wonderful. Adam and Eve loved God dearly and served him faithfully. This glorious situation continued till Satan tempted Adam and

Eve and they sinned, disobeying God, by eating the forbidden fruit from the 'tree of the knowledge of good and evil' (Genesis 2:9,16-17).

Sin ruined the world and all things in it, but we are told that when Jesus comes again he will remake the world as a perfect home for his people.

Reader, may it be that you have a place in that new creation.

Activities

a. Go outside and look up into the sky. Do this sometime during the day and at night.
b. Name some of the things you can see that God made.

God rules the universe

Read
Daniel 4

King Nebuchadnezzar said of our God: *'His dominion is an everlasting dominion, and His kingdom is from generation to generation. All the inhabitants of the earth are reputed as nothing; He does according to His will in the army of heaven and among the inhabitants of the earth. No one can restrain His hand, or say to Him, "What have You done?" '*
(Daniel 4:34-35).

One day I went to visit a member of my congregation, but when I arrived at his home, I was told that he had been called to work and that he expected me to visit him at his workplace. Now I knew that Leon worked at a sawmill, but I wasn't sure just what his special job involved.

It was a very hot day and I wasn't looking forward to going to a sawmill which had much machinery — and noisy machinery at that. I imagined it would be impossible to hold a conversation above all the noise. At first I thought I would go home and visit Leon another day. However, I had come a long way in the car and decided I would drive to the sawmill and speak to him. When I arrived I could see very large logs in piles everywhere. Very big machines were moving the logs down to the mill where they would be cut up by huge, sharp, circular saws. The work in some sections of the mill was very dangerous as every now and again we would read in the local newspapers of serious accidents happening. If someone was at all careless, it was easy to have a finger chopped off, or worse.

I asked some men to show me where Leon worked and they directed me to the very centre of the sawmill. One man said, 'When you get into the mill you will see a room near the saws. Leon works in that room.'

I made my way to the room and knocked on the door. I wondered if Leon would hear me as the noise was great, but he did and soon the door opened. When I entered the room I found it was air-conditioned — so different to the temperature outside. The room had great armour-glass windows through which Leon could see every part of the mill. There in front of his very comfortable seat was a big computer desk, covered with buttons and lights.

Leon was in charge of the mill section. He controlled the saws and the logs simply by pushing a button. He would touch one button and a large log would roll onto a long conveyor belt. Then the log would be taken to the big circular saws, which soon cut the log in half. Then with a touch of another button, another machine turned the log and it was cut again. Leon just watched what was taking place. He pressed the correct button and soon great logs became planks ready to be used for building. Leon was in charge of a great many machines that went to work when he decided that they should start. He controlled a large section of the sawmill.

I spent some time with Leon and much of the time was spent asking questions about his work and how the machines could do their job at the touch of a button. I went away amazed at what I saw.

As I was driving home I thought about Leon's job and was reminded of our great and all-powerful God. Our God created the universe through the Lord Jesus Christ. And then from his throne in heaven he controls every part of his creation — not by pressing buttons, but simply by speaking the word. Jehovah commands the angels to carry out his wishes. By his power the sun, moon, stars and planets float in space. By his power the earth spins on its axis.

By the word of his power the seasons come and go. Our God rules the whole of creation for his own glory and for the benefit of his people, who make up the living church of God.

Our God is all-powerful. And it is written of the Lord Jesus Christ, the Saviour of his people: 'All authority has been given to Me in heaven and on earth' (Matthew 28:18). The Saviour who loves us is the almighty God. This thought should give us true confidence to face, day by day, the difficulties which confront us. God rules the universe — not Satan — not man or woman, but God!

This thought should make us ever rejoice.

Activities
● ●

a. What are you going to do today?
b. Can you be sure you will carry out all of your plans? Why?
c. Why is it that God's plans always come to pass?

More precious than gold

Read
Psalm 19

'The law of the Lord is perfect, converting the soul; the testimony of the Lord is sure, making wise the simple; the statutes of the Lord are right, rejoicing the heart; the commandment of the Lord is pure, enlightening the eyes; the fear of the Lord is clean, enduring for ever; the judgements of the Lord are true and righteous altogether. More to be desired are they than gold, yea, than much fine gold...' (Psalm 19:7-10).

Gold is a very precious mineral. Every morning on the television when I watch and hear the news, there is a report about the price paid for gold. And its price varies almost every day. But the one fact that we all know about gold is that it is hard to find, it is hard to mine, and it is costly to buy. Many people like to wear jewellery made from gold, but such items are always costly. Other people like gold so much, they even have gold used for fillings in their teeth.

My brother John is not only a keen fisherman, he also loves searching for gold. Some years ago he purchased a gold detector and with several friends started to search for gold in one of the areas where it was found many years ago. They would look over the maps made by the early gold-miners and then drive to those areas and search for holes that had been dug many years before. Then with their detectors they would begin their search.

I remember the first time I had an excited phone call from my brother to tell me he had found a tiny piece of gold. He was so thrilled. He described his find and told me it was probably worth about $50.00. And he told me there was more where that piece came from.

Since then my brother and his three gold-mining friends have found quite a lot of gold. John has two detectors and between them they have purchased a tractor with a large blade on the front. With this machine they are able to scoop layers of the earth away and then detect lower in the soil for the precious metal. They even had a gold-miners' claim which they worked one day a week. They bought a back-end hoe to dig deep trenches looking for those precious pieces of gold.

Every birthday John sends me a small piece of gold which I hide away. Now and again I have a look at it. It is so shiny and just small pieces are worth a lot of money. Gold is very precious and there are many big companies mining vast areas of Australia looking for it.

There are also plenty of people who have their own gold detectors and they spend their spare time looking for the precious metal. These people work very hard. They have to walk over very difficult country and then have to dig up the soil with picks and shovels; most of the time they go home empty-handed. Every now and again there is a report in the newspaper of someone finding a large piece of gold. When this happens all the prospectors head out for the hills, hoping that they will discover the next valuable nugget.

Gold is mentioned many times in the Bible. Sometimes we read that people made their idols of gold and then bowed down and worshipped the god they had made with their own hands. In Revelation 21:21 we find a description of heaven and we read of the streets of the New Jerusalem — heaven: 'And the street of the city was pure gold, like transparent glass.' What a wonderful way to describe the city streets in the New Jerusalem! We know what our roads and streets are usually like — dirty and dusty with potholes. But not so in God's new creation. Everything there will be beautiful and precious.

The apostle Peter also uses gold as the way of describing true faith. He speaks of the genuineness of our faith as being 'much more precious than gold that perishes' (1 Peter 1:7). Reader, gold is precious, but it can be lost or stolen so easily. Our faith can never be lost. We think the things of earth are precious, but the things that are truly precious are the things of God.

Our text tells us something that is very true, and it is that God's Word, the Bible, should be very precious to every person. We know that the Bible is precious to every Christian for the Scriptures contain the teachings of our glorious God. The Bible points the way to Jesus Christ as the only Saviour of men, women, boys and girls. Truly the Bible is solid gold to every Christian because it contains the solid truth of God. The knowledge of the Scriptures makes God's people wise. Then as we read God's Word and find out how God requires us to live, the Bible becomes even more precious to us. In Psalm 119:127 the psalmist writes: 'I love Your commandments more than gold, yes, than fine gold!'

In some countries of this world, the Bible has been a hated book, and wicked men and women have tried to prevent people getting, keeping and reading God's Word. But courageous people have risked their lives to spread the Word of God about. Some have even been killed because they served God by reading and obeying his commandments. In our land we have great freedom to publish and read God's Word, but this might not always be the situation. So, reader, spend much of your time, not just reading your Bible, but committing it to memory. As you read and pray, you will come to realize that God's Word is the most precious book in the whole world.

We need to beware of 'fools' gold'. There is a mineral found in the soil that has a golden colour and looks just like gold. I can imagine some prospectors finding what they thought was gold. They would be jumping for joy, but when they examined what they had collected they would find it to be worthless.

24

In the world today there are many people who think that they will get to heaven by doing good works, by being a good husband or a good wife, or by attending church. All of these things are fine, but as far as salvation is concerned they are 'fools' gold' because they cannot save.

May every reader of this book know what true spiritual gold is — it is faith in the living Son of God, the Lord Jesus Christ, and living according to the teaching of that golden book, the Bible.

Activities

a. Make a list of precious things made from gold.
b. Why is gold so valuable?
c. What makes the Bible precious?

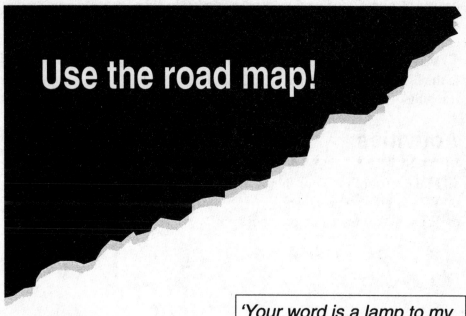

Use the road map!

Read
**2 Timothy 3:10-17
and Psalm 119:97-104**

I'm sure everyone likes to go for a drive in the car. It's fun to visit other places, but sometimes it is difficult to find our way to the spot we want to see. I remember once driving towards Sydney, the capital of New South Wales in Australia. Sydney is a very large city in which it is easy to get lost. But I was sure I knew the way to go. I had driven that way before and told my wife not to bother about the road map. I was confident that I could drive through Sydney without any trouble at all.

As we approached the outskirts of the city, my wife and I gazed at the tall buildings that were coming into view. The scenery was very beautiful as there were many fine homes surrounded by well-kept gardens. The flowers were very colourful and many graceful, tall trees and shrubs shaded the homes from the blazing sun.

Soon, however, I noticed that the traffic was getting thicker and I began to feel uncertain about the road I had to follow. The Sydney Harbour Bridge was looming ahead and there seemed to be roads going everywhere. Some streets were one-way and there were signs telling drivers to get into a particular lane if they wanted to reach a certain place in the city. I began to feel that I was lost. When that happens I usually get flustered, the palms of my hands begin to sweat and I keep a lookout for a place to stop the car. But this time there was no stopping-place. I was caught up in a line of traffic and I wasn't sure what I should do. So I just followed the car in front of me and hoped that it was going where I was hoping to go.

I said to my wife, 'Quickly, get out the street directory! Find out where we are and what road I must get into! Keep watching out for the road names!'

But my wife replied, 'Don't you remember! You said you knew the way and wouldn't need the directory. You put it in the suitcase in the boot.'

There was little I could do. I couldn't stop the car in the flow of traffic. I drove along very flustered until I was able to turn off into a side-street. I was hot and bothered, as I knew I should have had that road directory with us in the car. My wife would have had no problems directing me if only I had been more careful where I packed the directory. It took a long time to find out where we were and then it took a long time to find our way through the city. But with the road map we were able to navigate our way.

This story should remind us that as Christians we have a guide to tell us what we are to believe concerning ourselves and God. This guide is God's Word, the Bible, and this book instructs us how we are to reach the glorious destination which God has prepared for his people — that is, heaven. The Bible tells us that we can only reach heaven and our heavenly Father through faith in Jesus Christ. Jesus said, 'I am the way, the truth and the life. No one comes to the Father except through Me' (John 14:6).

The Bible is our guide — our 'road map' to heaven. We should therefore read the Bible and take note of God's directions concerning faith in Christ and living the life of holiness.

In our reading for today you will have noticed that Paul praised young Timothy for having learned the Scripture from his boyhood. In 2 Timothy 1:5 Paul tells us that Timothy had a godly mother, Eunice, as well as a believing grandmother, Lois. These two believers must have faithfully taught Timothy about Jehovah, the God of all creation.

It is a wonderful privilege to be born into a Christian family, for there you will be taught the wonderful truths of God. Christian parents and grandparents will pray for you. Mums and Dads know they have a great responsibility to teach their children the way of salvation. There are many wonderful stories in the Bible and there are many glorious truths that will guide us in our daily life. And as we get to know Jesus more and more we shall find our lives more joyful and satisfying.

Activities

a. Talk about a time when you were lost.
b. How did you feel at the time and how did you find your way back home?
c. How can you know you are travelling the right road to heaven?
d. What is the way to heaven?

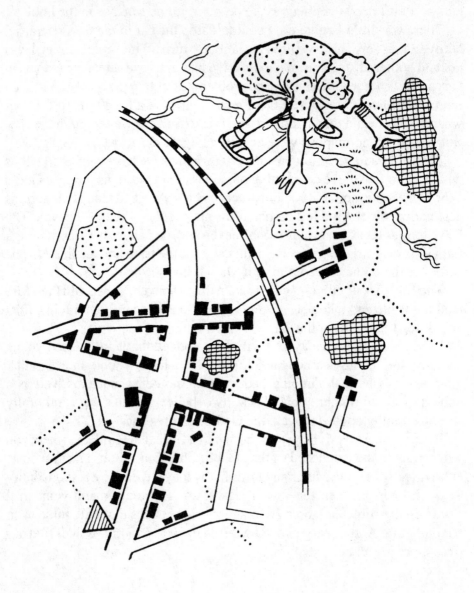

Beware of the devil!

Read

Isaiah 14:12-15

'Be sober, be vigilant; because your adversary the devil walks about like a roaring lion, seeking whom he may devour' (1 Peter 5:8).

The Bible has much to say about the devil, who is called Satan, or Lucifer. We read about Satan, the devil, tempting Adam and Eve in the Garden of Eden. We also know that when God had finished the work of creation he declared that all was 'very good' (Genesis 1:31).

If creation was so wonderful, how was it that the devil caused such a terrible catastrophe? Where did the devil come from and what made him become an enemy of God?

I'm sure that you have heard about 'pride'. There are many proud people in the world, and really we have nothing to be proud about. Everything that we are proud of is the gift of God. We might think that we can play cricket so very well, and boast to others of our great skill. But the truth is that we are only good at cricket because God gave us two good eyes to see the ball coming. He gave us the strength to play the game. No, really, there is nothing of which we can be proud. Everything and every ability we have is the gift of God.

Before Satan became the enemy of God, he was one of the most glorious of God's creatures in heaven — a most wonderful angel. As our reading tells us, he was 'Lucifer, son of the morning', or 'the day star' (Isaiah 14:12). Lucifer served God as one of God's creatures. But he became proud and decided that he was not satisfied with serving God. He wanted to push God off his throne and sit there himself. Now pride is a terrible sin and the Scriptures tell us, 'Pride goes before destruction, and a haughty spirit before a fall' (Proverbs 16:18).

In one town in which I once lived, there was a lady who was known for her pride. She was proud of everything about herself and her family. She was always boasting about herself and the things that belonged to her. She had the nicest car in the town. Her house was the tidiest. Her children never did anything wrong. She always dressed better than anyone else. She was always telling people how good she and her family were. The people in the town didn't like the woman very much. They were just sick and tired of her continual boasting.

One evening there was a special school function being held, and the parents were invited to a dinner. The Director of Education was to visit the school and give a talk to the teachers and parents. The town council and president were to be present. All in all, it was to be an important function. Everyone of importance would be there.

The proud lady of whom I have written was to be there as well. And as she walked into the school hall everyone looked at her. She was dressed in her very best. She even had on a small hat. Yes, she looked her very best and showed everyone how proud she was. She wanted to meet the Director of Education and while talking to him pretended she knew everything about education.

But as she boasted to the director, there was a little laugh behind her back.

Someone pointed to the proud lady, and there in her hair were two brightly coloured hair curlers. She looked so funny. The poor woman wanted her hair to look just the best, but forgot to remove the curlers before she left home. One of her friends soon took her aside and told her about the curlers. The poor lady nearly fainted. She felt so ashamed. The old proverb is so true: 'Pride goes before a fall.'

Pride was Satan's great sin. The Bible describes the beauty of Lucifer before he fell into sin. We read, 'You were the seal of perfection, full of wisdom and perfect in beauty. You were in Eden, the garden of God; every precious stone was your covering… You were on the holy mountain of God; you walked back and forth in the midst of fiery stones. You were perfect in your ways from the day you were created, till iniquity was found in you' (Ezekiel 28:11-15).

But Lucifer was puffed up with pride and we read in Isaiah 14:13-14 what he wanted: 'You have said in your heart: I will ascend into heaven, I will exalt my throne above the stars of God; I will also sit on the mount of the congregation… I will ascend above the heights of the clouds, I will be like the Most High.' Lucifer sinned by leading a rebellion against God's rule. He, Satan, was cast out of heaven and on earth, in his hatred of God, tempted Adam and Eve to sin by disobeying God's commands.

For a time, sin has ruined God's creation. But this will not be for ever. Through the saving work of the Lord Jesus Christ, God has rescued sinners from Satan's clutches. The day is also coming when Christ will return, and Satan and the demons who followed him in his rebellion will be cast into hell — the lake of fire.

When Christ came into the world, he overthrew Satan's power. Today

Satan's kingdom is under attack, people are being saved and won into the kingdom of God. However, our text tells us that even now Satan goes about like a roaring lion trying to cause people to fall into sin. He tempts Christians to sin against God. But, praise God, Satan can never drag God's people away from him. Today, Satan is a defeated enemy of God. When Christ returns, the whole world will see that this is true. It is God who rules this world.

Let us all beware of Satan. He is real and he is ever trying to take people to hell with him. Every day, read your Bible and pray that God will give you the strength to defeat Satan when he tempts you.

Reader, may God keep you safe from Satan's evil ways.

Activities

• •

a. Name some things which you are good at.
b. Is it right to be proud of those things? Why?

God's good gifts

Read
....
Luke 11:1-13

'Every good gift and every perfect gift is from above, and comes down from the Father of lights, with whom there is no variation or shadow of turning' (James 1:17).

The words above are wonderful words, because they tell a great truth, which is that God is the giver of good and perfect gifts. Perhaps sometimes when you have been given a gift you have found that you haven't been able to use it because something was missing. You may have needed a battery, or something was broken. But when God gives his gifts they are complete and nothing that we require is missing. The gifts of God are always suited to our needs.

God's creation was not just good, but God said that it was 'very good'. The creation was made for man and woman and suited the needs of Adam and Eve perfectly.

God's greatest gift was the gift of his Son, Jesus Christ. Jesus was exactly what sinners needed if they were to be saved. Jesus is both God and man in one person. As man he could represent his people in his life and death for sin. As God he could present to his Father his perfect sacrifice, and so open the doors of heaven for his people.

When I was reading the book of James in the New Testament, I came to our text and I remembered a terrible joke some fishermen played on one of their friends. I don't think they ever told him what they did or he would never have spoken to them again.

Some friends of mine loved fishing for eels. They would walk miles to a freshwater creek or river and fish for hours to catch eels. They loved the taste of eel. I never bothered fishing for eels as I thought the flesh was too tough, and catching eels meant a long and difficult walk through long grass. Also, eels had to be skinned and this was usually a messy job. One of the dangers of walking through the tall grass was that sometimes a snake would appear. And some snakes are poisonous. So I usually went fishing in sensible places.

Well, one day, before the men went fishing a friend asked them to bring him back an eel. Of course the fishermen said that if they caught enough they would drop one in to him on their way home. As the men were walking along they saw a movement in the grass. They stopped and watched. Suddenly a black snake lunged at them. In Australia the red belly black snake is one of the poisonous snakes, although a bite does not always kill the victim. Quickly the fishermen jumped out of the way and were about to run for their lives when one of the men grabbed a stick and killed the snake by hitting it on the head. They left the snake on the track and had a few hours' fishing. They caught several eels, skinned them and began to walk back home along the grassy track.

When they came to the dead snake, one of the men said, 'Let's play a joke on Graeme. He wanted an eel; let's skin that snake and give it to him. He'll never know the difference.' So the men set to work. They cut the head off the snake and skinned it. What was left looked just like an eel.

On the way home the fishermen called into their friend's home and gave him the 'eel'. Graeme and his wife were very pleased to receive that lovely gift from their friends. The next morning the two fishermen met again and they began to talk about their joke. Suddenly one of them said, 'I don't suppose the snake would make Graeme and his wife sick?'

'I never thought of that,' replied his mate. And then with a worried look they went to a phone. They thought they should tell Graeme of their joke.

When Graeme's wife answered the phone, one of the men said, 'Mary, that fish we gave you last night, I wanted...'

But Mary interrupted the caller and said, 'Oh, we wanted to thank you for that eel. We cooked it for breakfast today and it was so delicious. It was the best eel we have tasted. If you catch some more, don't forget to drop another one in.'

The fishermen thought it better to say nothing more. They decided it wasn't wise to confess what they had done. Theirs was not a good or perfect gift.

Jesus spoke about God giving wonderful gifts. We read his words: 'If a son asks for bread from any father among you, will he give him a stone? Or, if he asks for a fish, will he give him a serpent instead of a fish? Or if he asks for an egg, will he offer him a scorpion? If you then, being evil, know how to give good gifts to your children, how much more will your heavenly Father give the Holy Spirit to those who ask Him!' (Luke 11:11-13).

Reader, if you are not a Christian, you have here a very special promise, given by Jesus himself. He tells sinners that God is willing to give the Holy

Spirit to those who sincerely ask. When God gives the Holy Spirit to sinners, it means that they can truly trust in Jesus as their Saviour and Lord. It means that they have a living faith in the Son of God.

But you must ask, with all your heart and soul and mind, for God to bless you with his Spirit, and make you a new person, so that you will be able to follow Jesus faithfully.

Our gifts are never perfect, but God's gifts are both good and perfect. They are always exactly what we need to make us better Christians. And when God answers your prayers in some wonderful ways, and gives gifts to you, don't forget to give him thanks.

Activities

a. What is the most exciting gift you have ever been given?
b. What is the greatest gift that God gave to sinners?
c. Learn John 3:16 off by heart.

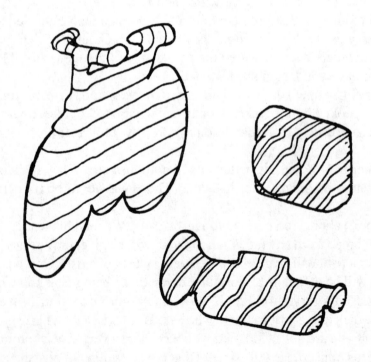

God's saving love

Read
. . . .
John 3:1-21

'For God so loved the world that He gave His only begotten Son, that whoever believes in Him should not perish but have everlasting life' (John 3:16).

This is the best-known verse in the Bible. It has been called 'the gospel in a nutshell'. This short sentence tells us of the great love that God has for his creation, a creation that rejected him as Lord and Master.

When God created this world, all was wonderful. There was no sin. God even met with Adam and Eve in the Garden of Eden, in the cool of the evening. It must have been a great experience for them to speak face to face with their Creator and God.

But Adam and Eve disobeyed God, even though God had told them that if they did not obey him they would die. By this God meant that death would come upon Adam and Eve in two ways. Firstly, their bodies would have health problems, age, and eventually die. Secondly, and more terrible, Adam and Eve would be cast into hell if they did not repent of their sins. Hell is called 'the second death' (Revelation 20:14).

When Adam and Eve sinned, death entered the world, and not just for those two, but for all their descendants after them. Sin is a horrible thing and we need to ask God to send his Holy Spirit into our hearts to show us just how wicked sin is. God would punish men and women for their sins, but he so loved the world that he sent his only Son, Jesus Christ, to die in the place of his people. The Bible tells us that 'Greater love has no one than this, than to lay down one's life for his friends' (John 15:13).

I would like to tell you a story about one person's great love for his wife. In the oceans surrounding Australia there are many dangerous animals. One of the most feared animals is the shark. With my brother John, I used to go out to sea fishing. In our small boat we would travel many miles from the shore and time and again we saw many very big sharks.

One day as my brother was pulling in quite a large snapper, he looked down in the water to see how big his fish was. He suddenly saw a huge shark diving up through the water, trying to catch the fish he was pulling in. John shouted out, 'Get the engine going! There's a huge shark coming towards the boat. Let's go for our life!' I remember trying to get that outboard engine going. It seemed to take a long time before it burst into power and away we began to move.

But John just held onto his line as he didn't want to lose his fish. Suddenly his line became very light and when we stopped the boat there was only the head of the fish left on the line. The shark had bitten off almost the entire fish. We were truly frightened that day. Even now when I have a swim in the ocean I make sure there are a lot of legs between me and the sharks that might be swimming beyond the breaking waves.

One night when I was listening to the television news, there was a report about a young couple — they had only just been married and were on their honeymoon. The lady was in tears and trembling as she told the story of her husband's death. They had gone diving in the sea to look at the fish and the very colourful coral that was found on the seabed. They were having a wonderful time, when suddenly a huge shark appeared. It began to show an interest in them and was between the two divers and their boat.

We can well imagine how frightened they must have been. Then the shark began to swim towards the young couple and they knew they were in for trouble. The shark came faster and faster and his teeth could be seen. The young husband loved his new wife dearly, and in an effort to save her life he pushed her out of the shark's way. And that was exactly what happened. During that attack his wife was able to swim to their boat and scramble to safety. But her husband was killed saving the young wife he dearly loved.

I was very saddened by this story, but I thought of the words I have already quoted: 'Greater love has no one than this, than to lay down one's life for his friends.' I also began to think of John 3:16, which speaks of the great love that God has for his sinful people. God loves this world, and God loves sinners.

I have told you about the bravery of the man who saved his wife's life. We know that he loved his wife. He also knew that she loved him. He did all he could to protect her. How wonderful it is that God loves sinners! He loved people who had broken his perfect law. He loved sinful people who hated him and wanted nothing to do with him. Jesus came into the world to save his people, and all who trust in the Lord Jesus Christ can say with the apostle Paul, 'I live by faith in the Son of God, who loved me and gave Himself for me' (Galatians 2:20).

We know that Christ, the Son of God, is God. In Isaiah 6:1-4 we have a picture of Christ before he entered the world. We read the prophet's words: 'In the year that King Uzziah died, I saw the Lord sitting on a throne, high and lifted up, and the train of His robe filled the temple. Above it stood seraphim; each one had six wings: with two he covered his face, with two he covered his feet, and with two he flew. And one cried to another and said: "Holy, holy, holy is the Lord of hosts; the whole earth is full of His glory!" And the posts of the door were shaken by the voice of him who cried out, and the house was filled with smoke.'

These words speak of God seated upon his throne, with the angels of heaven bowing before him. And how do I know that these words speak of the Son of God? Well, the apostle John, writing of the Lord Jesus Christ, said, 'These things Isaiah said when he saw His glory and spoke of Him' (John 12:41).

The Son of God loved his people so much that he came into the world to save them. He stepped down from the throne of his glory and came into this world as a baby. Throughout the entire life of Jesus, he perfectly obeyed his heavenly Father. He did this on behalf of his people. We couldn't obey God's commandments in order to be saved, but Jesus did so on our behalf.

And Christ died in a most horrible way upon a Roman cross. There he died in the place of his people, bearing their sins. He was punished by God for the sins of his people.

God loved his Son most dearly, and yet he sent him to bear the sins of sinners who hated him. How great is God's love for us! The apostle John tells us that 'We love Him because He first loved us' (1 John 4:19).

It is only when God sends his Holy Spirit into our hearts that we are given a love for him. If you love God and serve his Son then thank God for giving you a saving faith.

If you have no true love in your heart for Jesus Christ, and have no desire to serve God, then pray that God will not only show you your sins, but that he will give you the gift of faith and love for his Son.

Activities

● ●

a. How do you show your love for someone?
b. How did God show his love for his people?
c. How do you show your love for God?

We won the cricket!

Read
. . . .
Genesis 3:1-19
and 2 Corinthians 5:17-21

'*...in Adam all die, even so in Christ all shall be made alive*' (1 Corinthians 15:22).

In Australia most people love the game called 'cricket'. Children everywhere love to get out in a paddock, or on the road, put up some stumps (sometimes a waste bin), and play a game. Sometimes the players pretend they are the best cricketers of the day. Many young people practise cricket day after day, in the hope that one day they will play for Australia against other countries — especially against the British.

My wife enjoys watching the test matches on the television. I don't think much of cricket, but every now and again my wife calls out, 'Another one's out!' And when something very exciting takes place she calls out, 'Come and see this!' I usually get up and go to the lounge to watch the exciting part which is replayed at least three or four times.

But when the test match is concluded and the Australians defeat the British team, my wife calls out, 'We won!' And then on the television, in the newspapers and when people talk to one another about the test results, the word is, 'We won!' Sometimes, of course, the cry is, 'We lost!'

Now my wife and I didn't play in the test match, but we could say, 'We won!' because the eleven cricketers who made up the Australian team represented the people of Australia. When our team wins, we are so proud of our representatives.

When God created Adam and placed him in the Garden of Eden, he was the representative of all mankind. God would test his faithfulness and so told Adam that everything in the garden was for him, with the exception of the fruit of one tree, 'the tree of the knowledge of good and evil' (Genesis 2:17).

Our text tells us that because sinning Adam was our representative in the Garden of Eden, 'all die'. So, when Adam disobeyed God, and with Eve ate of the fruit of the 'tree of the knowledge of good and evil', his sin became our sin.

God has told us that 'The wages of sin is death' (Romans 6:23). With the exception of the Lord Jesus Christ, every baby who is born upon this earth is tainted with sin. King David wrote in Psalm 51:5, 'Behold, I was brought forth in iniquity, and in sin my mother conceived me.'

We have nothing to be happy about, because the sinful actions of Adam, our representative, made all of his descendants sinners by nature. His sin became our sin.

But our text goes on to say something about another representative of all of God's people — and that is the Lord Jesus Christ. Jesus Christ, the only begotten Son of God, came into this world to save sinners — to save all of those people who were given to him by his Father. Jesus came into this world as a baby, born without sin, because he, as our representative, was to live the life that Adam, Eve, and we should have lived. He was our representative before God, to live a life of perfect obedience to his Father. This he did for us.

Then, as our representative, he suffered the terrible punishment for our sins. Now, all who are 'in Christ' — that is, united to Jesus by a God-given faith — are saved from the anger of God, and are looked upon as righteous in God's sight, because our great representative did, on our behalf, what we should have done and could not do, because of sin.

Just as you can be happy because your team has won the cricket, the football or the baseball on your behalf, all of God's people can rejoice because the Bible tells us, 'The wages of sin is death, but the gift of God is eternal life in Christ Jesus our Lord' (Romans 6:23). This tells us what our text means by the words: 'So in Christ all shall be made alive.'

Isn't it a wonderful way of salvation? Christ loved his people from eternity — before they were born (Ephesians 1:4). He saved us by his actions. We cannot save ourselves, because we are unworthy sinners. There is nothing we can do to make God love us and save us. But because God loves his Son, who did all that was necessary to save his people, God loves those who live by faith in Christ the Saviour. And even the faith we need, to be 'in Christ' — even that is the gift of God!

Reader, if you are a Christian you should ever praise God who saved you through the gracious work of his Son.

Activities

● ●

a. When was the last time you said of your sporting heroes, 'We won!'?
b. How did Jesus represent his people whilst on earth?

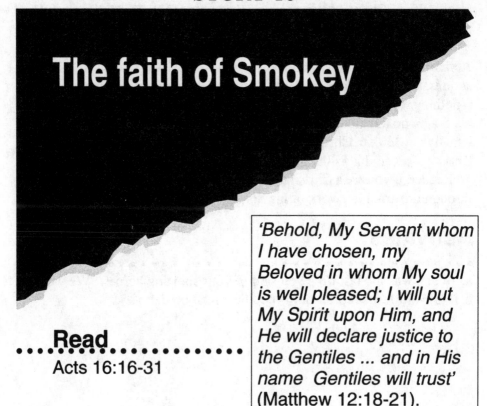

The faith of Smokey

Read
Acts 16:16-31

'Behold, My Servant whom I have chosen, my Beloved in whom My soul is well pleased; I will put My Spirit upon Him, and He will declare justice to the Gentiles ... and in His name Gentiles will trust' (Matthew 12:18-21).

Smokey, one of our many pet cats, was always getting into trouble and was ever expecting us to help in his time of need.

Some months after we were given Smokey, he began to climb trees. Now climbing trees is supposed to be easy work for a cat, but kittens begin by climbing small trees and then jumping down to the ground. We used to watch Smokey as he climbed the small lemon tree. He would run up the trunk and then play on the branches. It was great fun for him. When he was sick of playing in the tree he would simply jump down to the ground. He never seemed to know that he should climb down the tree trunk. But we knew that he would learn to do this one day.

One Saturday Smokey didn't come for his breakfast when he was called. The children became worried after some time, for Smokey always loved his breakfast of warm milk and some cat food. He also loved being patted on the head and rubbed behind the ears. In fact Smokey loved breakfast time so much he had learned to jump onto the window-sill of our daughter Lisa's bedroom and claw the fly-screen, hoping to get her out of bed to pay him some attention.

But this day Smokey didn't come when called. He was nowhere to be found. The children became very worried and began to search everywhere for the lost cat. After half an hour or so we heard the meowing of a cat and it seemed to be coming from far away. But when we began to follow the sound, we realized that the meows came from a tall tree across the road.

Sure enough, there was Smokey up the tree. It was a lot taller than the lemon tree that he was used to. He had climbed up the tree and was sitting on a branch high above the ground. That silly cat didn't know what to do to get down to the ground! He gazed down at us from his high perch. He tried to come down, head first, but then, filled with fear, would back up onto the branch. He seemed as if he wanted to jump down, but he must have realized that it was a long way to the ground and to jump would have hurt him. So there he sat on the branch, about five metres from the ground, and cried out for help. The girls were so upset, especially when I said, 'Let's go and have breakfast. He'll find his way down sooner or later!'

So what could I do? I wasn't going to climb up a tree to rescue a silly cat and we didn't have a ladder long enough to reach the branch. As we were walking home across the road to have breakfast I saw our waste bin, and lying beside it was a long piece of wood that I had used when doing some cementing. Here was the answer to the problem! Nail the waste bin to the pole and hold it up under the branch and hope that Smokey would jump in.

My wife said, 'Don't be silly! Smokey would never do that! He wouldn't have enough brains!' But the girls thought it was a great idea.

Soon we were under the tree and lifting the pole with the waste bin on the end. It was soon just under the branch where Smokey was still meowing. We called on Smokey to jump into the bin. Would you believe it? That cat trusted me so much that he really did jump into the bin.

There he was five metres above the ground in a waste bin nailed to the end of a pole. With his back paws on the bottom of the bin and his front paws resting on the top of the bin he just looked over the edge to see what would happen. Gradually I lowered the bin to the ground. As the ground came closer Smokey almost had a smile on his face. He was rescued!

But then a terrible thing happened. When the bin was about two metres from the ground, the nail which held it in place fell out, and Smokey rode the bin as it fell heavily to the ground. Just as the bin was about to hit the ground Smokey jumped! He landed on his feet and then raced as fast as he could across the road to the safety of the house. When we caught up with Smokey all he wanted was food and to be patted.

Reader, Smokey trusted us when we put the waste bin under the branch. He knew he was stuck up the tree and couldn't save himself. He simply didn't know what to do. We have a similar problem in that we are sinners and by ourselves we cannot get rid of our sins. But the Bible tells us that there is a way by which our sins may be removed, and that is by trusting in the Lord Jesus Christ as the only Saviour. The text at the beginning of the story says, '...and in His name Gentiles will trust' (Matthew 12:21). In our reading for today we read the words of the apostle Paul who said to the Philippian jailer: 'Believe on the Lord Jesus Christ and you will be saved...' (Acts 16:31).

Reader, when God shows you that you are a sinner, you will then know that you cannot get rid of your sins by anything that you might do. It is Jesus Christ alone who can save you. If you trust in him you will come to understand that he was punished by God for your sins — when he came to live on this earth and die that terrible death on the cross. Jesus was punished in the place of his people.

But we also need to be holy and we cannot become holy by anything we do, for we are all sinners. But again Jesus has done it all for us. He came to earth and lived as we should live. He obeyed God perfectly and he did this for his people. If you trust in Jesus for your salvation he will never let you down.

I don't think Smokey would ever again trust me with a waste bin when he got himself in trouble. I had really let him down! But Jesus will never let us down, for he is both God and man, and has all power in heaven and earth. He can save to the uttermost all who trust in him.

Activities

● ●

a. What is faith?
b. If you have a pet, how does your pet show his faith in you?

Faith — leaning upon Christ

> 'Who among you fears the Lord? Who obeys the voice of His Servant? Who walks in darkness and has no light? Let him trust in the name of the Lord and rely [lean] upon his God' (Isaiah 50:10).

Read
Matthew 11:25-30
and Luke 23:32-43

When Christ came to earth, he came to save his people from their sins. Jesus was afflicted, tormented, abused, deserted by his friends and finally put to death in a cruel way on a Roman cross. Yet in all of his distress, he trusted in God, for he knew that God would never leave him. Christ 'leaned' upon God and God upheld and strengthened him. Jesus trusted in God, and now Jesus says to weak sinners: 'You can lean upon me. You can trust God.'

When I was a schoolteacher I was involved in school camps. With other teachers we took a group of children to a camp beside the ocean and there we had a great time for five days. The children were involved in many games, craft activities and the study of God's creation.

One of the activities was to walk on a rope bridge, across a creek . There were just two ropes — one for the feet and the other for the hands to hold. The rope was old. In places it was frayed and looked as if it would break. None of the children was courageous enough to go across the rope bridge. They said, 'You go first, Sir!' I suppose they were hoping that the rope would break and I would fall into the water. However, I knew something they did not know. I made my way across the creek on the rope bridge. Then I returned to the children without any problems. The children were amazed that the rope did not break. However, I showed them that under the flax that looked so weak was a strong wire rope. It would not break. Soon everyone had crossed the river in safety.

Now, Isaiah tells us in our text that we can put our hope for salvation in Jesus Christ. We are so weak that we sometimes think we shall never reach heaven. Every day we sin by breaking God's law. But Jesus Christ is our great Saviour. In Christ dwells the fulness of God. He is the mighty saving God who has all power in heaven and on earth.

Faith in Christ is 'leaning' upon him alone for salvation. And because he is all-powerful he will save all of his people. Some people just try to save themselves by doing 'good' things, but the Bible tells us that no one can do anything that will cause God to save him. Jesus has done it all on our behalf.

Just think of that thief on the cross. What could he do to save himself? Nothing at all! He turned his head towards Christ and asked, 'Lord, remember me when You come into Your kingdom' (Luke 23:42).

I'm sure Jesus didn't look like a king when he hung upon that cross. Blood was pouring from his wounds. He wore a crown of thorns on his head. He was nailed to a cross and couldn't move. He looked so weak and powerless. But what faith was in the heart of that thief! He saw in Christ the only one who could save him from his sins. He realized that Christ was truly the Son of God, who had a kingdom. That poor thief simply trusted in Christ.

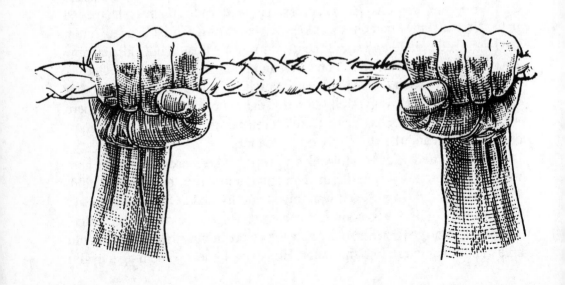

And what a wonderful reply came from the lips of Jesus: 'Assuredly, I say to you, today, you will be with Me in Paradise' (Luke 23:43).

Are you thinking: 'But I will sin again and again. I am weak!'? Tell Jesus of your doubts and fears and trust yourself to him, for he is strong and will certainly save all of his people.

Activities

• •

a. Of what are you afraid?
b. How did you overcome your fear?
c. Why do Christians 'lean upon Christ'?

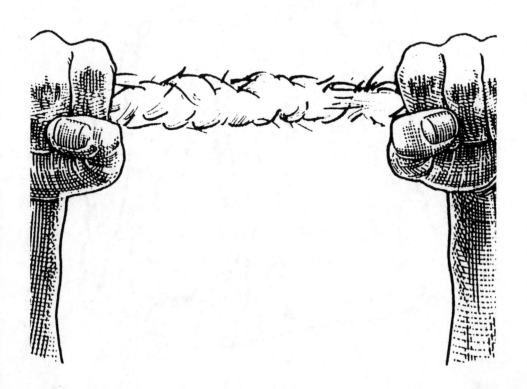

Faith — getting rid of our sins

...**Read**...............

Mark 4:35-41

'Cast your burden on the Lord, and He will sustain you' (Psalm 55:22).

At a very early age in my life I decided I wanted to be a schoolteacher. When I had completed high school, it was necessary to attend a teachers' college to study and to learn how to teach. Most of the young men and women who attended college had a scholarship and this meant we had some money to pay for board and our books. But we never seemed to have much money left over for clothes and for some entertainment. We were always on the lookout for holiday work in order to have some extra spending money.

One day I read in the local newspaper that quite a few people, especially women, were making a lot of money picking potatoes. This was at a time when there were many migrants coming to Australia. Usually both husbands and wives worked very hard to get ahead in their new land.

Now my friend Michael and I thought we would make a fortune if we worked during the holidays. The harder one worked, the more pay was earned. We thought that if women could make a lot of money, then we surely could make more. So we turned up at a farm one Monday morning and asked for a job. The farm owner was in need of more potato pickers, so we were told to start work at once.

It was a hot day, a very hot day, but we were young, in good health and thought all would be well. We had to walk along with a large bucket in one hand and bend over to pick up the potatoes from the ploughed land. Before long we found that the work was not as easy as we expected — our backs were soon aching. We were not used to this type of work. The women working beside us seemed to be doing a lot better job than we were. And they didn't complain about aches and pains.

When we had filled a bucket with potatoes, we emptied them into a potato bag. Now a potato bag is very big and when full, it is very heavy. The bags we filled had a tag on them, so at the end of the day we would know how many we had filled. Then we would be paid according to the work we had done.

During the day, every half an hour or so, the farmer would drive his tractor around and we would pick up our potato bags and put them on the trailer. At first we saw the ladies working together to lift their bags onto the trailer. It looked quite easy. But my friend and I found out that the bags were very heavy, and even when we helped one another it was hard to get the bag off the ground and onto the trailer. We felt as if our backs were broken. We were sunburnt and our legs felt so tired. Blisters were appearing on our hands. Picking potatoes was no easy job!

At the end of the day we collected our pay. It was not as much as we had expected, for we didn't do as much work as we had hoped to do. However, we thought that on the second day we would do much better. So home we went to have a warm shower, tea and then to bed.

The next morning, every bone and muscle in our bodies was aching, but soon we were at the farm ready for work. This time the farmer asked us to start the day off by carrying some bags of potatoes to a truck that would take them to the market. When I lifted the first bag to my shoulders I realized just how heavy they were. I took a few steps towards the truck and felt my knees starting to bend. The farmer knew what was about to happen and he ran over to me and said, 'Here, roll the bag onto my shoulder!'

What a relief it was! The weight was gone. My knees were no longer buckling under the weight of that bag of potatoes. I was not carrying the load any more, but the farmer was doing it for me.

Reader, our great burden is sin. Our sins weigh heavily upon us. They are so heavy that unless we get rid of them they will destroy us for ever. In our text we are told, 'Cast your burden on the Lord, and He shall sustain you' (Psalm 55:22). In these words we have a picture of saving faith. Our sins, our guilt and our shame are lifted from us and placed upon Jesus. Jesus says to his people, 'Here, roll your sins onto my shoulder. I will carry them for you.' By faith we roll our sins upon Christ, the sin-bearer. My sins, guilt and shame are now his to bear. And Jesus carried our sins, guilt and shame to the cross and there he bore our punishment. Our sins are gone and God says of the sins of his people: 'Their sins and their lawless deeds I will remember no more' (Hebrews 10:17).

In the New Testament we read a wonderful invitation made by Jesus to sinners: 'Come to Me, all you who labour and are heavy laden, and I will give you rest' (Matthew 11:28). Think of those disciples on the boat with Christ. The howling wind soon had the waves raging and the small boat was in

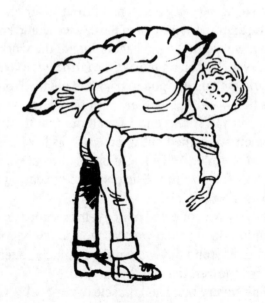

danger of capsizing. There was no doubt that death stared those disciples in the eyes. They turned to the only one who could help them in their distress. They called upon Christ and cast upon him the burden of their hopeless situation. You have read the outcome. Just a word and all was peaceful and quiet.

What a Saviour! And he invites you to roll the burden of your sins upon him, for he alone can deal with them. This he did 2,000 years ago on the cross at Calvary.

If you are still carrying your own sins they will crush you, for one day everyone must stand before the judgement-seat of God. All who are unrepentant sinners will themselves bear the anger of God and be cast into hell.

Saving faith is rolling your burden of sin onto Jesus and then living for his glory.

Activities

● ●

a. What have you tried to lift that proved to be too heavy?
b. How did you move the object?
c. How did Jesus rid us of our sins?

More about faith — safety in Jesus

Read
John 3:14-16
and Numbers 21:4-9

> 'Be merciful to me, O God, be merciful to me! For my soul trusts in You; and in the shadow of Your wings I will make my refuge, until these calamities have passed by' (Psalm 57:1).

I want to tell you another story that describes what faith is all about. Most young people today live in cities and have little idea about life on the farm. I grew up on a farm where we milked cows and had many animals. We had about ten fowls and there were always chickens in the fowl house. Every day we would let them out to roam about the paddock near our home. They loved finding grubs in the grass, and of course there was always plenty of seed there for them to eat. The hens also liked to have their daily bath. They didn't bath as we do, but they found some dirt and scratched the dust all over themselves. Then they would shake themselves. There they would stand in a cloud of dust, thinking they looked lovely!

But the mother hen always loved her chicks. She would ever be watching for danger. When the chicken hawk appeared in the sky, the chicks simply went on playing about, but mother hen knew there was real danger and would call her chicks to her. She would protect them from the hawk by spreading out her wings while they hid beneath. The chicken hawk found mother hen too big to attack and the chicks were safe.

One day when the chickens were out in the paddock a storm came up. The sky suddenly grew very dark and when we looked at the clouds there was a blue-green colour about them. That usually meant hail. But the fowls and the chickens didn't seem worried about the change in the weather. They just ate seed and scratched in the dirt.

Suddenly there was a flash of lightning and thunder roared overhead. Our dog didn't like storms so he ran to hide under the house. Then the heavens opened up and instead of rain, hail began to fall. Now, the hail was not very big — about the size of marbles — but they sure hurt when they hit. Mother hen realized that her chicks were in danger and she began to cry out to them. The chicks were being hit by the hail, so they ran to find safety under the outstretched wings of their mother. And there they were safe. The hail was falling on the poor mother hen whilst the chicks were kept dry and safe under her protective wings.

Then something terrible happened. A large hailstone hit the mother hen on the head and knocked her out. But the chicks were still safe, for they stayed under the outstretched wings of their mother.

Reader, faith in Jesus Christ means trusting yourself to him as your only Saviour.

You read in John 3:14-15 the wonderful promise made by Christ: 'And as Moses lifted up the serpent in the wilderness, even so must the Son of Man be lifted up, that whoever believes in Him should not perish but have eternal life.' It is Jesus we must look to if we would be saved.

If you have read the passage in Numbers 21, you will notice that those Israelites who were bitten by the poisonous snakes had only to look at the bronze serpent on the pole in order to live. Looking to Jesus for salvation means trusting in him alone for salvation. Looking to Jesus means following Christ's holy law.

God is angry with sinners and God will certainly punish all who are guilty of sin. But when you trust in Jesus he will protect you from the anger of God. He is like the mother hen who protected her chicks. The anger of God, which should fall upon all sinners, fell at Calvary upon Christ, who protects his people from God's wrath. In Psalm 57:1 King David said of his God, 'In the shadow of Your wings I will make my refuge.'

In the New Testament we read of Jesus, before he was crucified, looking over the city of Jerusalem and weeping. The Jews were God's covenant people. Jesus had come to save them, but they wanted nothing to do with him. Christ knew that soon the wrath of God would fall upon the people and the city of Jerusalem. He wept for his people and said, 'O Jerusalem, Jerusalem, the one who kills the prophets and stones those who are sent to her! How often I wanted to gather your children together, as a hen gathers her chicks under her wings, but you were not willing!' (Matthew 23:37).

Today Jesus invites sinners to come to him for salvation, to trust in him to protect them from the wrath of God. You are called to put your salvation in the hands of Jesus Christ who is 'able to save to the uttermost those who come to God through Him' (Hebrews 7:25).

Are you trusting in him?

Activities

• •

a. From what dangers does Jesus protect his people?
b. How does Jesus protect his people?

56

Confessing Christ

Read
Matthew 5:1-16

'Therefore whoever confesses Me before men, him I will also confess before My Father who is in heaven. But whoever denies Me before men, him I will also deny before My Father who is in heaven' (Matthew 10:32-33).

Many times in the Bible we are commanded to bear witness in our lives to the saving work of the Lord Jesus Christ. Jesus told his hearers that God's people were 'the light of the world' (Matthew 5:14).

Light has one use, and that is to drive away darkness. And sin is darkness. So as Christian people we, by our words and lives, are to let the world know that we belong to Christ. We must be able to say with the apostle Paul, 'I am not ashamed of the gospel of Christ, for it is the power of God to salvation for everyone who believes, for the Jew first and also for the Greek' (Romans 1:16). All of God's people, young and old, boys and girls and men and women, are to act in such a way that Christ is honoured and people are pointed to him. Everyone needs to be warned that Christ is going to return to judge the world in righteousness.

The very first school at which I taught was a place called Iron Pot Creek. Iron Pot Creek was away out in the bush. It was just a one-teacher school with about twenty children, ranging in age from five to twelve years. I had just finished my college course and was hoping for a school in a small village, but my school was about thirty kilometres from the nearest town. To get there I had to travel by train for about fourteen hours and then catch the daily post van to the school. It was a lovely little school and the people in the area were very nice; but it was so isolated.

When I arrived, one of the first things I wanted to know was why Iron Pot Creek was so named. I was told that in the early days of the British settlement of Australia, the settlers moved up the eastern coast and then moved inland. The land was good, but very heavily timbered. It took a lot of hard work to make a farm in Australia in the early nineteenth century. As the settlers moved into new areas they weren't too sure whether the Aboriginals would be friendly or not, so when camp was made each night, someone used to keep watch in case of an attack.

A group of settlers once reached a nice valley with a creek running through and thought it would make a good farming area. They decided to make their camp near a bend in the creek, and as everyone was tired after a day forcing their way through the bush, they made their beds and were soon ready to go to sleep. But who was going to keep watch during the night?

One of the men said, 'We're all tired, so what about tying the dogs about the camp. They'll be sure to bark and cause a fuss if anyone is sneaking about.' As no one really wanted to sit up and keep watch, the dogs were tied up in different positions around the camp.

A fire was soon alight and the men began to cook a meal in a great big pot which they hung on a chain over the fire. The meal was delicious, but as the men were tired they decided to leave the washing of their cups and plates — and the cooking pot — till morning. Then the travellers settled down in front of their fires for what they hoped would be a good night's rest.

Everyone was soon asleep, but towards midnight a dog began to make a terrible noise. He was barking and howling, both at the same time. The men jumped up in fear, thinking they were being attacked. They grabbed their guns and hid behind trees looking at the spot where the dog was making all the noise. The dog still barked and howled in what seemed terror. As the men looked harder into the night they saw the dog in the dim firelight.

Then they saw what was causing all the fuss. The dog had broken the rope that held him to the tree and, as he could smell the leftover food in the cooking pot, he had come to have a feed. When he put his head into the pot it became stuck. No wonder he began to yelp, bark and howl in fear. That dog was useless as a watchdog. His message was all wrong.

But this is not to be so with Christ's people. We are to tell the world by our words and deeds that we are Christians. We are to shine as God's people in this sinful world. We must never be ashamed of all that Christ has done for us. When he carried our sins to the cross, he carried our shame, but he was not ashamed to live and die for all who would follow him.

So, reader, you must live in such a way that others 'may see your good works and glorify your Father in heaven' (Matthew 5:16). And when the opportunity presents itself you should speak to others about Jesus and what he has done for you.

Jesus has made a very special promise to all who love him and confess him before the people of this world: 'Whoever confesses Me before men, him will I also confess before My Father who is in heaven.' This is part of our text for the day. What a wonderful promise that will be fulfilled perfectly on the Judgement Day! Jesus will tell his Father that all who have trusted him belong to him and they will never perish, but enter the wonderful new creation that God has prepared for his people — the new heavens and the new earth.

How do you know that your faith is a saving faith? The answer is very simple! Christ's people obey his commandments and one of his commandments is to confess him before men. To whom then must you confess Christ? It is to your schoolmates, your playmates, your brothers and sisters, your mother and father, the people next door. You don't have to become an overseas missionary to confess Christ. Christians are called to be ambassadors for Christ just where they live.

The reading for today tells us of the character of God's people. Simply living the way Christ would have us live is one wonderful way to confess Christ before our friends and neighbours.

May God use you to win someone into his kingdom.

Activities

• •

a. How do Christians let other people know that they love Jesus?

b. Are you a Christian?

The power of the gospel

Read
Acts 9:1-19

'For the message of the cross is foolishness to those who are perishing, but to us who are being saved it is the power of God'
(1 Corinthians 1:18).

I am sure that my readers have heard of dynamite. Dynamite is an explosive that has a lot of power. When I was young, farmers used dynamite to blow large tree stumps out of the ground. In some places they still do this! They would dig a hole under a tree stump, and then place a stick of dynamite, with a fuse attached, well down in the hole. The hole would be covered in. When everyone was well out of the way, the fuse would be lit and the person would run for his life and hide behind a tree for safety. The explosion would blow the stump out of the ground without any trouble at all.

I even heard of some people who would take a stick of dynamite to a water hole in a creek or river, light the fuse and throw it in. The explosion that resulted would kill fish and make them float to the top of the water. It made fishing very easy!

When I was teaching, I taught at a small country school for several years. This was not Iron Pot Creek, but — would you believe it? — it was called Repentance Creek. It was there that I became a Christian! The farmers there had to round up their cattle every two weeks and take them to a very big cement dip, where the cattle would be forced to swim through water in which there was a potent poison that would kill cattle ticks. These cattle ticks would harm the health of the animals and sometimes kill young calves, so the Department of Agriculture had decided to try to totally eradicate cattle ticks from that part of the country. The farmers were not happy about what was to be done. It meant rounding up the cattle and driving them to the dipping area every two weeks. They also claimed that dipping meant the cows would not produce as much milk as beforehand.

Despite the farmers' opposition, the government workmen brought in their bulldozers and cement trucks and soon had a very large cement dipping area. It seemed as if the cement was metres thick. It looked as if nothing could move the dipping yard. But one night, some of the farmers crept down to the dip and placed sticks of dynamite about the cement trenches, and blew it up completely. The dynamite proved that it was a very powerful explosive. The use of dynamite could change the landscape.

In our text today, the apostle Paul tells us that the 'gospel', the good news concerning salvation in Christ, acted like dynamite in the lives of many people. In Paul's age the gospel changed lives, just as it does today. The Greek word that Paul used in our text (translated 'power') is the word from which we get our English word 'dynamite'.

The apostle Paul knew that there was great power in the gospel of Christ, for he had been a proud Pharisee, who had done all that he could to destroy the Christian faith. He had gone about rounding up the followers of Christ, putting them in jail, having them whipped. We read in the Bible that he had held the coats of the men who stoned Stephen to death (Acts 7:58; 8:1).

But when the Lord Jesus spoke to Paul on the road to Damascus, he was

62

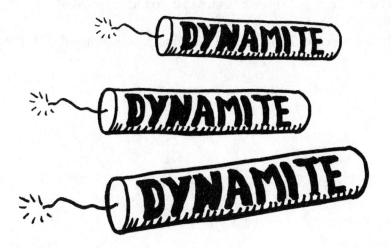

changed. The Holy Spirit transformed Paul's life in a very wonderful way. He felt the power of the gospel in his life. Now Paul became a Christian and he himself was locked up in jail, whipped and finally put to death because of his love for the Lord Jesus Christ. Many, many people have had their lives changed because of the 'dynamite' — the power of the gospel.

I know of people who were drunkards, being changed by God's Holy Spirit in such a way that they were never the same again. Instead of hurting their families, they loved their families because they were filled with the love of God and became followers of Jesus Christ.

Our God is ever ready to forgive the sins of all who ask him to do so — provided they are sincere in what they say. Then by the grace of God they begin to live lives of obedience to him. Even the most wicked people can be saved when, by the power of God, they repent of their sins. The Bible tells us that Jesus 'is also able to save to the uttermost those who come to God through Him...' (Hebrews 7:25). Even the very worst sin can be washed away in his precious blood. The prophet Isaiah spoke of the wonderful cleansing power of God. We read, '"Come now, and let us reason together," says the Lord, "though your sins are like scarlet, they shall be as white as snow; though they are red like crimson, they shall be as wool"' (Isaiah 1:18). There is true saving power in the gospel of Christ, and that good news is for sinners.

Reader, the gospel is for you! Pray that God will show you the power of the gospel, by sending his Holy Spirit into your life. Like the apostle Paul, if that happens, you will become a true servant of Jesus and so inherit the kingdom of heaven, that Christ has prepared for all of his people.

Activities

a. What is the most powerful thing that you have heard of?
b. What can that thing do?
c. If there is power in the gospel, has that power changed your life yet?

Silly sheep

...**Read**...............
John 10:1-17

'And let us consider
one another in order to
stir up love and good
works, not forsaking
the assembling of
ourselves together, as
is the manner of
some...'
(Hebrews 10:24-25).

I once taught at a small school called Tilbuster. The school was situated in an area where many people were graziers. There were sheep in thousands dotted across the hillsides and plains. It was once said of Australia that the country rode on the sheep's back. The greatest export for many years was wool. So sheep were important. Graziers bred the best sheep possible and Australian Merino wool was, and still is, some of the best in the world.

Sheep move about in flocks, and sometimes there are thousands moving about together. There is safety for the sheep when they keep close together, as in Australia there are dingoes, wild dogs, that kill sheep. They usually pick out a sheep or lamb that has strayed from the flock and attack and kill it for their evening meal.

Something else that we enjoyed at Tilbuster were the blackberries. Now blackberries grow on vines that are covered with thorns. It is hard work picking a bucketful of these delicious berries. Gloves are needed to protect the hands. Sensible people always wear long trousers, a long-sleeved shirt as well as good, strong boots. Blackberry pie, with ice-cream, made the scratches from the vines all worthwhile.

However, the blackberry bushes were always a problem to straying

sheep. I guess the grass beside the vines always looked greener and more delicious to some sheep. Many times a sheep would move away from the flock and go off by itself to feed beside the blackberry vines. But blackberry vines easily become entangled with the wool on the sheep, so often the silly wandering sheep would find itself caught firmly in the vine. The more it struggled, the more entangled the sheep would become.

One day, as I was looking for some blackberries, I heard a sheep bleating close by. I thought I had better find out what the trouble was, and soon found a sheep well and truly entangled in a blackberry bush. The flock of sheep was several hundred metres away, grazing safely. Apparently this one sheep thought it would do better for itself if it left the flock. After some pulling and struggling, I was able to drag it free from the vine. I let it go. Without a bleat of thanks, the sheep looked at the flock, and ran back as quickly as possible. With the flock the sheep was now safe and secure.

There is a real lesson for every Christian in this story. How many times do we hear of people who appeared to be faithful Christians drifting back to their old sinful and godless ways? What usually happens is that they begin to wander away from the gathering of the church, just as the sheep left the flock. They miss worship. No longer do they attend Sunday school or the Bible studies. After a while they disappear from the church scene. They are caught up in the affairs of the world and unless the Lord is gracious and brings them to repentance they go on in their sins and finally are lost for ever in hell.

Our text tells us very clearly that we are not to forsake the gathering of God's people. It is with God's people we are taught the truths of Scripture and together we encourage one another to go on with Christ as his faithful people.

We must also be wary of false teachers who would try to entice us away from God's people and lead us along a pathway that leads to hell. Our reading encourages us to follow Christ faithfully, and not to be led astray by godless people. The Bible tells us to keep together with the people of God, for Christians help their brothers and sisters in Christ to move along together, in safety, worshipping and serving Christ.

Reader, have you fallen into the blackberry vine of the world, the devil and the desire to please yourself? Have you turned your back on Christ and his people to go it alone in the world? If this is so, then get back with the flock and repent of your sins, and together with God's people get on with the joyful life of loving and serving Christ.

Activities

a. Why do you like mixing with your friends?
b. Why do Christians get together so often?

And the cat came back

Read
• •
Luke 15:11-32

'But the father said to his servants, "Bring out the best robe and put it on him, and put a ring on his hand and sandals on his feet. And bring the fatted calf here and kill it, and let us eat and be merry; for this my son was dead and is alive again; he was lost and is found." And they began to be merry' (Luke 15:22-24).

Our children always had pets of one kind or another. Once there was a dog. Then there were guinea pigs, a bird, some mice, but most of all there were cats.

The most loved cat was one they called 'Smokey'. Smokey loved the good things of life. He just loved being fed and lazing about in the warm sun. And the children loved him. They were always playing with him and giving him a wonderful time. Smokey, however, had one very bad habit. He loved climbing into the car, through an open window, and then lying under the rear window, where the sunshine gave him great warmth. For Smokey, this was the good life.

He wasn't always able to get into our car, so was ever on the lookout for cars parked near our home. When he spotted one he would walk around it looking to see if a window was open. If he found one, he would jump through and settle down in the sunshine under the rear window. Sometimes, if a truck was parked nearby he would jump in the back, find a warm, soft place and then go to sleep.

One morning a Telecom truck pulled up beside our home and the workmen began to do some repair work on the telephone lines. Smokey saw his chance and was soon on top of the truck, nestling down on some rags that had been left between the rungs of a ladder. In the warm sun he soon fell asleep.

Later the workmen returned to the truck, as they had finished their work. They hopped in and drove off, with Smokey still on top. His love of the good, easy life was to cause him awful trouble. A child, who was waiting for the school bus, saw what had happened and called out in great excitement: 'Sir, your cat has just gone off on the top of that truck!' And when the children heard that they became very upset and Cathie, who always claimed that Smokey belonged to her, began to cry, 'Smokey's gone. We'll never see him again! He'll be killed!'

So I hopped into our car and headed off in the direction that the truck had gone. The workmen weren't in a hurry to get to their next job, so I finally caught up with them. I blew the car's horn several times and the driver brought the truck to a standstill.

'What's the matter?' the driver asked.

'Our cat has just had a ride on the top of your truck,' I replied. One of the men hopped out and climbed onto the back of the truck, but no Smokey was to be found.

I drove home to tell the children the sad news. And as I drove along I kept watching for that silly cat. His bad habits had really caused him trouble this time. But there was no cat to be found on the side of the road. So with saddened hearts the children went off to school that day. When they arrived home from school that afternoon, there was still no Smokey to be found.

But after several days, Smokey came back! And what a mess he was in! He couldn't walk properly, and bits of skin and hair were missing from his body. He must have jumped, or fallen from the truck as it sped along. The poor old cat! But how pleased the children were! They hugged Smokey. Then they gave him warm milk to drink and made a lovely soft bed for him to rest in till he recovered. For several days Smokey was treated with tender loving care and was nursed back to health.

Some Christians are like Smokey. They get caught up in the life of the world and begin to drift away from Christ. They begin to make their home in the world and start to live for self and pleasure, and this is sinful. But, like the Prodigal Son in today's Bible reading, they find out that sin is not at all pleasant. In this parable Christ told of a wayward son — the son who wanted his inheritance in advance, so that he could leave home and live it up in the world. He sinned greatly against God and his father. In fact, he ended up in a pigsty. But he repented and went home to his father. And how he was welcomed home!

Christians backslide — they get lost in their spiritual life; but Christ always brings his people home. And wayward Christians always come back with true sorrow in their hearts because they have sinned against God. Smokey walked home in his own strength, but when Christians get lost, Christ, by his Spirit, draws them home to himself.

When Smokey returned home he was battered and bruised, and till his dying day he carried the scars of his truck ride. When Christians fall into sin it can be very painful, for God chastens his people, so that they might learn their lesson and remain faithful to him all the remainder of their lives. Chastening hurts and there are times when sin leaves terrible scars. Smokey never bothered about cars and trucks from that day onwards. He learned how foolish he had been.

Great promises are made in the Scriptures to all of God's people. In Jude 24 we read these wonderful words of comfort: 'Now to Him who is able to keep you from stumbling, and to present you faultless before the presence of His glory with exceeding joy, to God our Saviour, who alone is wise, be glory and majesty, dominion and power, both now and for ever. Amen.'

Activities

a. How do you think you would feel if you were lost?
b. How do you think the Prodigal Son felt when he was met by his father?
c. Why did the father forgive his wicked son?
d. Why does God forgive his sinful people?

I enjoy Kentucky Fried Chicken

Read

John 10:7-30

> 'My sheep hear My voice, and I know them, and they follow Me. And I give them eternal life, and they shall never perish; neither shall anyone snatch them out of My hand. My Father, who has given them to Me, is greater than all; and no one is able to snatch them out of My Father's hand. I and My Father are one' (John 10:27-30).

I really enjoy the taste of Kentucky Fried Chicken. I think it is the best cooked chicken in the world. Whenever my wife and I are out driving, she says I can smell the Kentucky Fried Chicken shop miles away. When passing such a shop I sometimes say to my wife, 'Is it all right to stop and get some chicken and fries?' But the reply usually is: 'Remember your waistline!' Of course I just drive by without complaining too much.

One day my wife and I went for a drive and we agreed that we should stop at the first Kentucky Fried Chicken shop and buy a meal. I was overjoyed and my taste buds were thrilled. After a short time we came to a K.F.C. shop, went inside and ordered a delicious meal. We decided to eat our food in the car which we had parked on the roadside. The meal was very appetizing. When we had almost finished, we noticed a dog, a small fox terrier, trotting along the pathway. He had his head up in the air and seemed to be sniffing the lovely smell coming from the Kentucky Fried Chicken shop. Suddenly he stopped, for we could see that he had noticed a bag lying near the path. I'm sure he thought to himself: 'There's a meal for me in that bag.'

Over he went and began to push his nose into the bag. Sure enough, in that paper bag there were some bones thrown away by an untidy person. That dog was surely happy. He tried to get the bone out of the bag, but it seemed stuck. He pushed his nose further and further into it. Soon his head was so far in that his eyes were covered up, and he couldn't see what was going on around him. But he wanted that bone, and must have decided he would take it home to eat it there. So he began to make his way to the side of the road, with just one eye peeking over the top of the paper bag. Every now and again, even that one eye was covered. The fox terrier simply couldn't see the cars coming and going along the road.

But the dog wouldn't release that bone. He stepped out onto the road and a car raced by, blowing its horn. Back he jumped, but he still wouldn't let go of that bone, even though he was risking his life.

We just sat there and watched, hoping that the dog would safely cross the road. After several attempts, with just part of one eye looking over the top of the bag, he moved out. He was listening for cars and soon made it to the middle of the road. Then he heard a car coming. He shook his head so that the bag moved and he could see that it was safer to stand still for a moment. When the car passed, he raced to the other side of the road, his teeth still gripping that Kentucky Fried Chicken bone. The last we saw of the dog he was safely trotting along the path on the opposite side of the road. He still couldn't see very well, but he was heading towards his home with the bone securely held between his teeth.

This reminded both my wife and me of the way in which the Lord Jesus Christ deals with his people. When Jesus sends his Spirit into the heart of a sinner and makes it possible for that person to repent of his sins and trust in him, he declares that for ever that person belongs to him. God's people are safe and secure for all eternity. No one can snatch his people away from him.

Satan tries to tempt the repentant sinner to live for himself and the thrills of the world, but Jesus hangs on to his friends. When people in the world try to win us away from Jesus, they can't do it, because he has his hands about us. Our security is in the fact that Jesus has hold of us. If my security depended upon my hanging onto Jesus, I would not be safe, for I am weak. But Jesus is strong and so we are safe eternally. Thus Jesus could say with all confidence about his people: 'And I give them eternal life, and they shall never perish; neither shall anyone snatch them out of My hand' (John 10:28). The apostle Paul put it this way: 'I am persuaded that neither death nor life, nor angels nor principalities nor powers, nor things present nor things to come, nor height nor depth, nor any other created thing, shall be able to separate us from the love of God which is in Christ Jesus our Lord' (Romans 8:38-39).

Once God has sent his Holy Spirit into our hearts, we are changed in our natures. The Bible tells us that we are a 'new creation; old things have passed away; behold, all things have become new' (2 Corinthians 5:17).

God will never let his people perish. This is an amazing truth. God will keep us faithful. Everything in our salvation depends upon God. He has promised to save his people. He always keeps his promises.

Activities

●●

a. What makes you feel safe at home?
b. In what way does the devil try to turn his people away from Jesus?
c. How is it that Jesus can keep his people spiritually safe?

Melted teeth

Read
Luke 12:16-21

'Come now, you who say, "Today or tomorrow we will go to such and such a city, spend a year there, buy and sell, and make a profit"; whereas you do not know what will happen tomorrow. For what is your life? It is even a vapour that appears for a little time and then vanishes away. Instead you ought to say, "If the Lord wills, we shall live and do this or that." But now you boast in your arrogance. All such boasting is evil' (James 4:13-16).

I'm sure that all fishermen exaggerate when they talk about the size of the fish they caught, or they tell you about the big one that 'got away'. Some of the children in my class at school thought I exaggerated when I held my hands apart and told them how big were the fish that I had caught. Several of the boys then found a piece of three-ply wood and cut two holes in it — the holes were about ten centimetres apart. They gave me the plywood one morning when I started to tell them about the big fish I had caught on Saturday. They said, 'Sir, this is a "whopper stopper". Before you tell us about your fish you have to put your hands through the holes in this wood. Then you can't exaggerate about how big the fish were.'

I laughed with the rest of the class at their joke, so I put my hands through the holes and said, 'On Saturday I went fishing out to sea and caught some very big fish. They were so big!' I couldn't move my hands in the 'whopper stopper' to show the children how big the fish were so I just said, 'The fish were so big that their eyes were this far apart!' I moved my hands as far as I could in the 'whopper stopper'. The children got the message that the fish were big, and everyone had a good laugh.

Well, I'd like to tell you a true story about several friends of mine who decided to go fishing for trout. They were schoolteachers and it was holiday time. Stewart and Ian loved fishing and they had planned a four-day fishing trip during the winter vacation. They talked about the trip they would make, and spent a lot of time getting their gear ready. They were going to camp in a tent near a small river, where there were always plenty of trout to be caught. They caught some small frogs and had plenty of worms for bait. They also had some food with them, but not too much because like all good fishermen they said, 'We'll catch plenty of fish. We'll cook and eat them.' Their wives decided they would not go on the fishing trip as it was cold weather, and they liked their warm beds too much.

At last Stewart and Ian were ready to leave. They had their trailer attached to the back of their car. It was loaded with everything they thought they needed for their much talked about fishing trip. They had even told all their friends about the big fish they were going to catch. So sure were they of catching a lot of fish, that they took a car refrigerator with them. They had made their plans. They had forgotten nothing. It was going to be a great few days' fishing.

The men were soon waving goodbye to their wives and children and they headed off down the road to their special fishing spot. It took several hours to reach the river, where they soon put up their tent, sorted out their fishing gear, made their beds and gathered wood for the fire they were sure would be needed to cook their fish.

Darkness was soon about to fall, so they decided they would catch some fish for tea. They gathered their fishing gear, lit their lanterns and headed over to a deep hole in the river. Soon they had caught several very large trout.

'I told you we'd catch some fish this time,' said Stewart.

'Yes,' replied Ian, 'the girls will be really proud of us. We're sure to have a load of fish to take home.'

Ian and Stewart decided they had caught enough fish for tea that night and walked very proudly back to their tent. Soon they had a fire burning and a panful of fish gently sizzling. They thought the smell of the fish cooking was really appetizing. They couldn't wait to sink their teeth into that beautiful white fish flesh.

As the flames blazed up about the frying pan, a spark from the fire dropped into the fat in which the fish were frying. Suddenly the whole pan of fish burst into flames. Stewart knew what to do. He grabbed the pan handle, lifted the frying pan from the fire and blew at the flames with all of his might.

Now, Stewart had false teeth and — would you believe it? — he blew his teeth out of his mouth. They landed in the flames in the frying pan. His false teeth just melted in the fire. And when the fire in the pan died down, Stewart and Ian didn't know what to do. They had made such careful plans for their fishing holiday. They had done everything they could to ensure it would be a fishing trip to remember — and it was!

Without his teeth Stewart could not eat. The men didn't want to pack up and go home, but they had to, for Stewart now needed a new upper plate of teeth before he went back to school. All of their plans came to nothing!

And this happens so often to us also. We make our plans and boast about what we will do. But we must always remember the words of our text, which tell us quite clearly that God rules our lives. Truly, we make our plans, but we never know what the day might bring forth. When we make our plans we should always say, 'We will do this or that, if *the Lord wills*.' Always remember the parable of the 'Rich Fool' found in Luke 12:16-21. Jesus there spoke of a man who had much wealth. He built bigger barns for his crops and eventually said to himself, 'I will now retire and enjoy myself.' But God said to that foolish man, 'You fool! This night your soul will be required of you' (v. 20).

All that the man had saved he lost, because he died. Jesus is teaching us that the riches of this world cannot save anyone. That which saves is spiritual riches, which is faith in the Lord Jesus Christ. This salvation is shown in the life we live loving and serving our great Saviour, Jesus Christ.

76

Reader, the Bible warns us that *today* is the day of salvation. Jesus invites us to believe in him now. Tomorrow may never come for any of us. Tonight you may die. Now is the time to call upon Jesus to put his Holy Spirit in your heart and give you the gift of faith and the ability to repent of your sins. May God bless each one of you.

Activities

● ●

a. What plans have you made that didn't come to pass?
b. Why should you become a Christian today and not leave it till next year?

Making choices

Read
Romans 8:28-39

'Blessed be the God and Father of our Lord Jesus Christ, who has blessed us with every spiritual blessing in the heavenly places in Christ, just as He chose us in Him before the foundation of the world, that we should be holy and without blame before Him in love...' (Ephesians 1:3-4).

We are always making choices and some choices are hard to make. When I go to town, at lunch-time I often have to choose between a chocolate malted milk shake with a large scoop of ice-cream, and a cup of tea for drink. I know what I would like to have. But I know what my wife thinks is best for me, because she just pats me on the stomach. She doesn't even have to say a word for me to know what my choice ought to be.

Two of my grandchildren each had a pet rabbit. They had faithfully looked after their pets for four years. They fed them each day and cleaned out their hutch. They played with them and every now and again let the rabbits out of their cage for a run in the backyard. Of course the rabbits soon found out where the lettuce grew and always headed for the garden patch.

One morning when the children went out to feed their pets, all they could find were a few lumps of fur. They never found their rabbits and I guess a dog must have attacked them during the night. Scott and Jessica were heartbroken. They just cried and cried for a long time.

Then one morning at about seven o'clock our phone rang and their mother Heather was on the phone, asking if I would go with her and the children to pick out two new rabbits. They had heard a radio announcer saying that a person had some young rabbits to give away. The children had begged their Mum and Dad to be allowed to get one each. I had the job of going along to help make the choice. They wanted to get two mother rabbits or two father rabbits — not one of each.

When we arrived at the place where the rabbits were, the children were so excited. They ran to the cage, and the owner said, 'Take your pick. Just tell me which baby rabbit you want and it's all yours.'

I didn't have any opportunity to help make a choice. Jessica saw a lovely little grey rabbit and said, 'I'll have that one, please.' It didn't take Scott too long to pick out his baby rabbit as well. They just chose the rabbit they loved best of all. Home we went and the baby rabbits were placed in a new and safer hutch. No one knew whether they had picked a mother and father rabbit. (Since then the rabbits have had several lovely baby rabbits of their own. Grandfather is very popular with Scott and Jessica!)

I'm sure you have made many decisions in your lifetime, as has everyone. When we make a choice we usually pick the thing that appeals to us, the thing that looks best and will be best for us. The Bible tells us that God has chosen a people to be saved. We are also told that Jesus Christ, the Son of God, died to save those people alone. Our text tells us that God chose a people for salvation before the foundation of the world. This truth is very hard for us to understand, but it is the truth of God's Word.

All humans are sinners. We love our sins, and by nature we want nothing to do with God, or his Son, Jesus Christ. The apostle Paul, writing to the church at Rome, tells us what our nature is really like. He wrote, 'There is none righteous, no not one; there is none who understands; there is none who seeks after God ... there is no fear of God before their eyes' (Romans 3:10-18).

Paul is here telling us that humans love their sins so much they will never, if left to themselves, repent and go to Christ for salvation. We would never choose Christ as our Lord and Saviour. So all of us would be justly cast into hell for our wickedness. But the Bible tells us that God is a God of love. To show that love he chose a people whom he would save from their sins.

Now I know that when I make a choice, I pick what I think would be best for me. The reason for my choice is in the thing I choose. But this is not the case with God's choice of his people. He did not choose the best-looking people to be saved, or the richest, or the best behaved. For some reason, known only to God himself, he made the choice of a great number of people to be saved from hell. He set his love upon these people before the world was created. The Bible tells us, 'We love Him because He first loved us' (1 John 4:19).

God chose a people to be saved. Then he made it possible for them to be saved. God sends his Holy Spirit into the hearts of his people, and so changes them that they begin to love Jesus and hate their sins. God gives his people the gift of faith, by which they are able to trust in Christ for the forgiveness of their sins, and for their salvation.

God's people don't earn their salvation. Left to themselves they would be for ever lost in hell. Jesus Christ, by his life and death, has earned the salvation of his people. If you trust in the Lord Jesus Christ you should love God more and more and praise him louder and louder for all that he has done for you. You should thank God for sending his only Son to die for you. You should thank God for sending the Holy Spirit into your heart and giving you the gift of faith. Everything concerning our salvation has been done for us by a loving and gracious God. We choose God, because he first chose us. He has written the names of his people in the Book of Life (Revelation 13:8; 20:15).

Some people might tell you that if God has chosen a people for salvation, then there is no hope for you, because you might not be one of his chosen people. Reader, believe this great truth. Jesus said, 'All that the Father gives Me will come to Me, and the one who comes to Me I will by no means cast out' (John 6:37). The invitation of God to sinners is, 'Believe on the Lord Jesus Christ, and you will be saved' (Acts 16:31).

This is all we need to know. If you begin to show an interest in Christ and salvation then believe that it is God who has given you that interest. Then pray that God will totally change your heart and give you the gift of saving faith. Believe what Christ said in the passage of Scripture above: 'The one who comes to Me, I will by no means cast out.' Then, with all your heart and soul and mind, trust in Christ for your salvation. Repent of your sins and live the life of obedience to Christ. Jesus said, 'If you love Me, keep My commandments' (John 14:15).

When we witness to others about the love of God in our lives, we do not say to ourselves, 'Maybe this person has not been chosen by God. Could it be that I'm wasting my time speaking of Christ to this person?' What should be in our mind is this: 'God has a chosen people in the world. It is possible that the person I'm talking to is one of God's people. Maybe at this very minute God is using me to tell this person of God's great love. Could it be that he (or she) will have his heart changed as I am speaking?'

Left to ourselves no one would be saved, but praise God there is a people who will believe, and if you are trusting in Christ for your salvation, then praise God for his great goodness to you.

Activities

● ●

a. Name three things you have chosen this week.
b. Why did you choose those things?
c. Why do sinners choose to follow Christ?

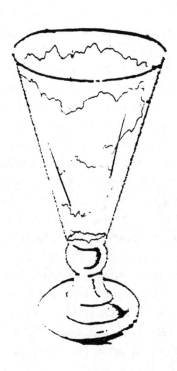

A day in court

Read
· ·
Jeremiah 23:1-6

> '*...that He might be just and the justifier of the one who has faith in Jesus*' (Romans 3:26).

I would like to try to explain to you what is meant by the biblical word 'justification'. There is a catechism for young people called *The Shorter Catechism* and question 32 asks the question: 'What is justification?'

Putting the answer in my own words, 'Justification is an act of God's free grace, wherein he pardons all our sins, and accepts us as righteous in his sight, only for the righteousness of Christ, which is put to our account and received by faith alone.' This is hard to understand, for the word justification is a legal word which means to declare that a person is righteous.

I'm sure you have seen court scenes on television and probably know how a court works. When I was young I didn't know much about courts and how they worked until one day I had to appear in a court. I was a witness for a boy who had been punched in the nose by a bus conductor. This boy was a friend of mine and we were travelling home on the school bus. Some children were misbehaving and causing the conductor a lot of trouble. Suddenly something happened and the bus conductor turned around, and in anger punched my friend right on the end of his nose. My friend was innocent, and was punched by mistake. But his nose was broken and his father and mother were very upset about the incident. His father decided to take the matter to court.

One day I received an official letter telling me to be in court on a certain day. I was to give evidence, telling what had happened. I was only thirteen years old, and I was very afraid of what would take place.

On the day, I sat in the court and the judge was there on his bench. There were two solicitors, one representing my friend and the other representing the bus conductor. After some speeches were made, several witnesses, including myself, were called, and after we promised to tell the truth we were questioned about the incident. The judge found the bus conductor guilty and he had to pay my friend's medical expenses, as well as the court costs. That was my only time to take part in a court case and I didn't like it very much at all.

Our God has demanded that all humans be holy as he is holy (1 Peter 1:16). We also read in the Bible, 'Pursue peace with all men, and holiness, without which no one will see the Lord' (Hebrews 12:14). We all know that we are guilty sinners. How, then, is it possible for men, women, boys and girls to be saved? How is it possible for God to consider us to be holy people? How is it possible for God to 'justify' a sinner? This is how it is possible.

From the Bible and my stories, you know that Jesus came into the world to save his people. He did two things for them. First of all, he lived a perfectly holy life, on behalf of his people. He did what his people could not do. He lived without sin.

Secondly, he died upon the cross as our sin-bearer. Jesus took the sins of his people from them and placed them on himself. Then God punished Jesus as if Jesus was the sinner. Christ was the one who suffered on behalf of his chosen people. The Bible tells us that when a sinner believes in Jesus Christ as his Lord and Saviour, he is 'justified'. That is why the sinner is considered perfectly holy by God.

I want you to imagine a court-house in heaven. Down on earth there is one of Christ's people, for whom he lived and died. That sinner is 'born again' by God's Holy Spirit and is now able to say, 'I trust in Jesus for my salvation!' At that moment in heaven something wonderful takes place.

Imagine the court sitting in heaven. God is sitting upon the throne of judgement and the sinner who has just believed in Christ is mentioned. There in the court are those who will bring evidence against the sinner. God's law says, 'That sinner has broken the law and we all know that the wages of sin is death. He should be cast into hell.' Satan says, 'Yes, that sinner is mine. He is an unholy person, and we all know that without holiness no one can enter heaven.' Even the sinner's conscience says, 'Yes, I know that I've broken God's law and deserve to be cast into hell.'

So, it appears as if the sinner has no hope. He is truly guilty of breaking God's law and should be condemned. But before God can pronounce the sentence, someone stands up and speaks on behalf of the sinner. This person, Jesus Christ, is the true representative of the sinner. And Jesus declares, 'That sinner belongs to me. On that sinner's behalf I lived a life of holiness. And that sinner cannot be punished for his sins, because I am his sin-bearer. I carried his sins to the cross and there I was punished on his behalf.'

Then it is as if God the Judge looks through Christ at the sinner on earth. What God sees is the holiness of Christ around the sinner. No longer does God see the sinner's sins because now the sinner has new clothes on — clothes made from the spotless righteousness of Christ. God the Judge pronounces the believing sinner to be forgiven and righteous in his sight, and that for the sake of the saving work of Jesus Christ.

Even though the believing sinner is still on earth and, sad to say, still breaks God's law, God has declared that for the sake of Christ he looks upon the sinner as legally holy in his sight. Justification is the sentence of the Judge: 'Not guilty!' The sinner is justified through faith. And saving faith is the gift of God and is the link between God's people and Christ.

Reader, do you see that our salvation is only to be found in Jesus Christ? It is truly said of our Saviour that he is 'the Lord *our* righteousness' (Jeremiah 23:6).

Our justification takes place in the court of heaven, the moment we trust in Christ. We are not present in that court, because we are still on earth. But because of Christ's saving work and the gift of faith that fills our hearts, God now looks upon us differently. No longer are you seen as a sinner to be cast into hell, but as a person clothed in Christ's righteousness and as truly being a citizen of heaven.

We should ever sing the praises of our Saviour God.

Activities

• •

a. Why do your loved ones forgive you when you do something wrong?
b. Why does God forgive sinners?

No more cheesecake!

Read
. . . .
Luke 19:1-10

'Then Peter said to them, "Repent, and let every one of you be baptized in the name of Jesus Christ for the remission of sins..."' (Acts 2:38).

It was the day of Pentecost, fifty days after the Passover, at which time the Lord Jesus Christ had been crucified. The Holy Spirit had been given to the church in a new and more wonderful way than ever before. The apostle Peter 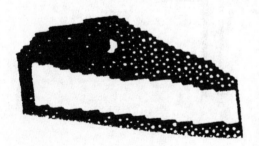 had just preached a great sermon to the many people who had gathered at Jerusalem to celebrate the Feast of Pentecost. He had reminded the people of the great crime that had been committed, when Christ had been crucified. No doubt, some of the people who heard Peter speak had been among the crowd who had cried out, 'Crucify Him! Crucify Him!' (John 19:6) when the Roman soldiers were preparing to put Jesus to death.

Some three thousand of those who heard Peter preach that day realized what a terrible thing they had done. They came to understand that they had been involved in the killing of Christ, the Son of God. These listeners were ashamed of their sinful action and knew that God would judge them for their sin. They cried out to Peter and the other apostles, 'Men and brethren, what shall we do?' (Acts 2:37). Peter's reply is our text for this story.

Peter told his hearers that first of all they had to repent of their sins. Now what does the Bible mean by the word 'repentance'? There are two types of repentance. One is a true sorrow for breaking God's law. The other is just being sorry you were caught doing something wrong — not being sorry for doing the wrong thing.

A long time ago I was nice and thin, but when I married, my wife proved to be a wonderful cook. As the years went by I found that my waist was getting bigger and bigger, I had to buy new and larger clothes every now and again. My wife Valerie kept telling me that I would have to lose weight or I'd become ill. After twenty years of her asking me to get rid of my excess weight I started a diet and began jogging.

Soon I was 'Slim Jim' again and my wife was very happy. Even my doctor was surprised and praised me for losing the weight. I was also very pleased with myself.

I kept the weight off for about five years, but I developed a very bad habit. During the night I would wake up and very quietly slip out of bed, go to the refrigerator and have something to eat. Valerie knew what was happening and she would say to me, 'You've been at the refrigerator again. If you're not careful you'll put all that weight back on again. And you know how hard it was to take it off.'

For a few nights I would behave myself, but then I would be up again and off to the refrigerator. I was always so quiet as I was ashamed of what I was doing, and I didn't want Valerie to know I was eating during the night.

I love cheesecakes, with cream and strawberries on the top. One night before bed I saw a cheesecake in the refrigerator and I thought to myself, 'If I wake up tonight I will eat that cheesecake. Then before Valerie misses it, I will get to the shop and buy another one and replace it. She'll never catch me out.'

Sure enough I woke up and had a wonderful meal of cheesecake. I put the packet it was in into the waste bin and thought I would not be found out. However, just before we were to sit down and have breakfast, Valerie opened the refrigerator and noticed what was missing. 'You've been at it again,' she said, looking hard at me. 'You've eaten that whole cheesecake I was defrosting for our tea tonight!'

What could I say? I was well and truly caught out. I hung my head down in shame and said, 'I'm sorry. I won't do that again.' I didn't really mean it, and my wife knew. 'You're not truly sorry,' she said. 'If there was another cheesecake there tonight you'd eat that too.' And I knew my wife was right in what she said. I was just sorry my wife missed the cheesecake before I could replace it. My sorrow, or repentance, was worth nothing!

The apostle Paul wrote about my type of sorrow. He said to the Christians at Corinth, 'For godly sorrow produces repentance to salvation, not to be regretted; but the sorrow of the world produces death' (2 Corinthians 7:10). There are many people who pretend they are sorry for their sins, but really they are only sorry that their sins have been found out. A thief is not usually sorry that he has stolen money, but rather is sorry that the police have caught him and he might go to jail. He might say, 'I'm sorry. I'll never steal again!' But what the thief really means is that next time he steals, he'll be more careful, and won't be caught. That is not what the Bible means by repentance, or godly sorrow. Repentance is to know in your heart that you have done something wrong and what you have done is to break God's law. It is to realize that in the first place you have offended God. If the thief is truly sorry that God is offended by his actions, and he is truly sorry that he has stolen someone's goods, this is the first step in true repentance. The thief must say to himself, 'I hate what I have done because I have broken God's law.'

The next step in repentance is to decide that by the grace of God we will not sin again. Of course we do sin again, but when we do, we will be ashamed of ourselves and ask God to forgive us.

In my own words, the *Shorter Catechism*'s answer to question 86, 'What is repentance unto life?', describes true repentance like this: 'Repentance to life is a saving grace, whereby a sinner, having a true sense of his sin, and an understanding of the mercy of God in Christ, turns with grief and hatred from his sin to God with full resolve and effort after new obedience.'

Our reading today was about a man named Zacchaeus. This man understood what repentance involved for we read his words to Christ: 'If I have taken anything from anyone by false accusation, I restore fourfold' (Luke 19:8). If we have by our actions caused harm to someone we will put it right. We will apologize to the person we have hurt. If we have stolen someone's goods, we will return them. If we have said cruel and hurtful things about someone we will tell the people we have spoken to that what we said was a lie. We will show true sorrow. Maybe there will be real tears in our eyes when we repent.

King David, the second king of Israel, committed some terrible sins. He stole another man's wife and then had the man killed so he could marry the woman. It took some time before David was truly sorry for his terrible sin, but when he repented, he did so with great sorrow. He wrote Psalm 51 which speaks of his sorrow and repentance: 'I acknowledge my transgressions, and my sin is ever before me. Against You [God], You only, have I sinned, and done this evil in Your sight' (vv. 3-4). Then he wrote, 'Purge me with hyssop, and I shall be clean; wash me, and I shall be whiter than snow... Create in me a clean heart, O God...' (vv. 7,10).

If we would be saved by Christ, then we must truly repent of our sins. And we cannot repent of our sins until God puts his Holy Spirit in our hearts. Reader, if you have not repented of your sins, then plead with God to send his Spirit into your heart, that you might repent and find forgiveness through Christ.

Activities

● ●

a. Have you ever felt sorry for doing something wrong? Why?
b. What should we do when we have broken God's law?

Money to burn!

Read
• • • • • • • • • • • • • • • • • • • •
Luke 12:16-34

'Do not lay up for yourselves treasures on earth, where moth and rust destroy, and where thieves break in and steal; but lay up for yourselves treasures in heaven, where neither moth nor rust destroys and where thieves do not break in and steal. For where your treasure is, there your heart will be also' (Matthew 6:19-21).

I'm sure that every one of you has some special object that you really treasure. But, when you consider the thing you treasure so much in the light of eternity, it isn't that important after all. Some years ago I saw a person with a lovely gold Sheaffer biro. I thought to myself, 'If I can ever afford one of those I will buy it.' When my wife and I visited Singapore I saw one for sale in the airport. We were soon to board our plane for Australia, so I raced over and purchased it. I took great care of it till I arrived home. Then my wife asked me, 'That biro you bought? What are you going to do with it?'

I thought that to be a silly question and said, 'I'll use it every day.'

But my wife replied, 'You lose every biro you take around with you. This one will be gone before you know it!' I thought for a while and knew she was right. What then was I to do with my great treasure?

Well, my gold biro, which I like so much, is safely hidden away, where I hope no one can find and steal it. The only time I ever take it out is when I conduct a wedding ceremony. I allow the bride and groom to sign their wedding certificate with it. And when I die, if I still have my golden biro, someone else will get it, use it and probably lose it. The things we treasure on earth will be left behind when we die. Old Job spoke a great truth when he said, 'Naked I came from my mother's womb, and naked shall I return there' (Job 1:21).

There are some people who believe that we can take our treasures with us when we die. I'm sure you have read about the Pharaohs in Egypt who were buried with their possessions. They thought those things would be of use to them after death. When my wife and I were in Asia we visited a temple. It was a very colourful place and we were able to walk about and watch what was going on. There were priests at work. Some were lighting incense sticks. Some were praying. But the priests who gained my special attention were those who were involved in cutting paper in the shape of money. They wrote something on the paper, then they took the bundles of paper and burned them. The smoke from their fire curled up throughout the temple.

I went to our guide and asked, 'What are those priests doing over there?' He replied, 'They are making money and then burning it, because they believe they are sending money to the dead who are in another world.'

We all have things we treasure on earth. We build strong banks to protect our treasures. Some people have strong safes in their homes to protect their valuable items. Some put burglar alarms in their homes for protection, and today, more and more, we see homes with strong bars protecting the window spaces. But when we die we shall leave everything behind us. You never see a hearse on its way to a cemetery, pulling a trailer full of the dead person's possessions to be buried with the dead body. God has been very good to us, for he has provided us with so much to enjoy. But our earthly treasures are not the important ones.

Jesus told a parable about a rich man who had enough money and possessions saved up that he decided to retire, and take things easy for what he hoped would be a long time. He said to himself, 'Soul, you have many goods laid up for many years; take your ease; eat, drink, and be merry.' But all was not to be well for that man, for we read, 'But God said to him, "You fool! This night your soul will be required of you; then whose will those things be which you have provided?" So is he who lays up treasure for himself, and is not rich toward God' (Luke 12:19-21).

How true it is — earthly treasures don't last! What lasts is the treasure God's people have in heaven. That treasure is safely put aside for us and will be there when we finally enter into the presence of God. Our text tells us that in heaven there are no moths to eat our valuables; there are no thieves to steal our heavenly treasures, and our treasures will never rot or rust away in God's heavenly safe.

What, then, are these treasures which are stored up for us? First there is a life with Christ that will never come to an end. Then there is the love of God, which is in our hearts now and will never be lost. There is the perfect righteousness of Christ for us to be clothed in. And we shall inhabit a new heaven and earth, which is perfect in every respect. Indeed, Jesus has told us that he entered heaven to prepare mansions for his people (John 14:2).

Another great treasure is the faith which we have in Christ. That treasure is given to God's people here on earth. That will last for ever. And what a wonderful treasure it will be, to be reunited with our loved ones who died in Christ! We shall meet them again and enjoy their company for ever.

The greatest treasure of all awaits God's people when they enter the gates of paradise — Jesus will be there to welcome us to our home. Many heavenly treasures Christians have here and now, but more glorious and lasting treasures are still waiting. They are stored up in heaven, just waiting for us to arrive and receive them.

There is nothing sinful in having treasures while we live on earth; but we must always understand that God has given them to us, to be used for his glory. We are not to hug our treasures to ourselves, but to use them to help the spread of the gospel, or to assist people who are in need.

Reader, may you remember what Christ said to that rich young ruler, who loved his riches more than anything else. He wanted eternal life. He tried to keep the commandments, but we read Christ's warning to him: 'If you want to be perfect, go, sell what you have and give to the poor, and you will have treasure in heaven; and come, follow Me' (Matthew 19:21).

That rich young man loved his wealth more than Christ. He loved the things of the world more than God. He needed to be born again in order to see that the only treasures that really matter are the heavenly ones.

May God give each one of you who reads these stories the gift of faith that you might have the treasure that is so important — heavenly treasure that will last for ever.

Activities

● ●

a. What is the most precious thing you own?
b. For how long do you think it will last? Why that long?
c. What are some of the treasures God has prepared for his people?

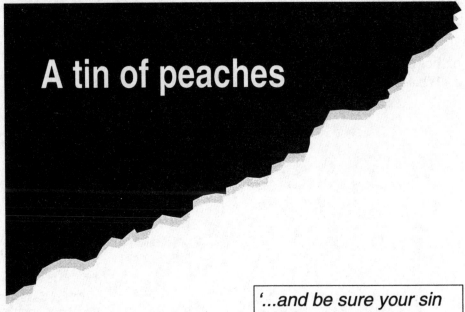

A tin of peaches

Read
....
Joshua 7

> '...and be sure your sin will find you out' (Numbers 32:23).

It is hard to imagine a world in which there is no such thing as tinned food. But I can remember a time when fruit was bottled by my mother. It was always great fun on the farm when we helped Mum gather the fruit for preserving in bottles. Only on very rare occasions was there any tinned fruit in the cupboard.

One afternoon when my brother and I arrived home from school, we found six tins of peaches in the pantry. We had never seen so many tins of fruit before. And we always loved tinned fruit. Mum and Dad were milking the cows and we had the opportunity to steal a tin of peaches. We decided that we would take one tin out to the haystack and eat the lot. We knew that this was wrong. We needed to ask permission to eat the peaches, but we thought that as there were six tins, Mum would not notice that one was missing.

So my brother and I took the tin of fruit with a can opener, and climbed up on the haystack where we couldn't be seen. There we opened the tin and ate all of the peaches. They were lovely! But we had an empty peach tin which would be the evidence that we had stolen the peaches. We decided that we would throw it down behind the haystack. No one would ever find it there.

My brother and I then went home and began to do our school homework. Our stomachs were full and we were very happy.

But an hour or so later we heard a shout from outside. It was Dad: 'Come out here, you two boys!' Out we went, without a care in the world. But there at the foot of the steps was Dad with an empty peach tin in his hand. We were speechless. We were sure that no one could ever have found the empty tin. 'Did you boys take this tin of peaches from the pantry?' Dad demanded. There was nothing we could say because we were guilty.

'But how did you find the tin?' we asked. 'We hid it behind the haystack.'

Then we noticed that Dad's hat was on the ground, and it was half full of eggs, some of which were cracked.

'You fellows didn't know about the hens laying eggs behind the haystack, did you?' Dad replied. 'I found the tin in the nest and some of the eggs were broken.' We hung our heads as Dad began to take off his leather belt. Our sin had caught up with us, and there was no way out. Never again did we steal peaches. We had learned our lesson. Our sin had found us out!

Today there are so many people who believe they can break God's law and that God will never know about it. Crimes are committed in secret. Sometimes crimes are committed and the guilty people are never found. They think they have escaped punishment. But let us remember the words of Scripture at the start of this story: 'and be sure your sin will find you out'.

I trust you have read the story of Achan in Joshua 7. Here was a man who would not obey God. He stole what did not belong to him and hid his treasure. I'm sure that he and Mrs Achan thought that no one would discover what they had done. But in this instance, their sin was revealed and they were punished in a most horrible way.

If our sin is not discovered in this world, we must remember that there is a day coming when we shall all stand before the judgement-seat of Christ. If we are not saved, cleansed by his shed blood, then our sins will rise up to condemn us.

Let us beware of sin. God's eye is upon us. Let us all live in such a way that Christ is glorified.

Activities

● ●

a. Think about some terrible thing you have done which nobody knows about.
b. Will it be a secret for ever? Why?

Trapped! Sin brings its own punishment

Read
• • • • • • • • • • • • • • • • • • • •
1 Samuel 24:1-7

'They have prepared a net for my steps; my soul is bowed down; they have dug a pit before me; into the midst of it they themselves have fallen' (Psalm 57:6).

The psalm that our text is taken from was written by David, who was to become king of Israel. The king of that day was Saul, who hated David so much that he wanted to have him killed. David was forced to escape from King Saul and hide wherever he could find safety.

In our reading we find David hiding from Saul. During the night he was able to creep up to the sleeping Saul and cut off a piece of his clothes. David could easily have killed Saul.

In Psalm 57 David speaks of wicked men who were out to trap him: 'They prepared a net for my steps...' But these advisers put King Saul in such a situation that he could have been killed and so trapped in his own net.

I always try to watch the evening news on the television. It was that time of the day when I asked my family to be quiet for an hour so I could watch in peace and quietness. The girls often complained that the news was 'not interesting'! Sometimes they would make noises playing games, and I would have to ask them to be quiet. One of my daughters, Vicki, who complained the most, is married and has her own children. Now she tells her children to be quiet so she and her husband can listen to the news.

One night the newsreader gave a report about two men who broke into a railway station in order to steal money from the stationmaster's safe. The door to the office was very strong and they couldn't force it open. The robbers then decided to break a window and enter that way. Soon they were in the office and somehow were able to open the safe. They grabbed the money and set fire to the building before they left. They thought the building would burn down and no one would know that there had been a robbery. They were sure that they were very smart thieves.

The men had petrol with them, so they put some papers under the stationmaster's desk, which was near the broken window, threw the petrol around and dropped a lighted match on the heap. Now while the thieves were robbing the safe a secret alarm went off, notifying the local police that a robbery was taking place. The police were on their way to the railway station.

Well, the match was thrown onto the petrol-soaked papers and desk, and there was a great 'Whoosh!' as a sheet of flame flashed about the room. Then, much to their horror, the two thieves could not get to the broken window to escape. Without thinking, they ran to the door to make their escape, only to find it bolted hard. They were trapped by their own wickedness.

I watched the television report with great interest, for a reporter had accompanied the police to the railway station. He had taken a video film of the events. The report showed the smoke coming out of the stationmaster's broken window. Then I could hear the sound of the thieves inside screaming out for help.

The policemen soon had the door broken open with the help of an axe they carried in the police car. Then out staggered the two thieves. Both men's clothes were burning and they were screaming out in pain. One policeman was seen grabbing a fire hose, and soon water was gushing over the two men as they lay on the ground writhing in terrible pain. The fire brigade soon arrived accompanied by an ambulance.

When I saw and heard this report it made me think of God who hates sin. We are told in the Bible that all men, women, boys and girls who do not trust in the Lord Jesus and repent of their sins will be judged by God and cast into hell. There they will remain for ever as a just punishment for breaking God's holy law. But there are times when God punishes sinners whilst they are still on this earth. The Bible tells us that God hates sin and that 'God is angry with the wicked every day' (Psalm 7:11).

In 1 Corinthians 11:17-34 we read of people who were sinning at the Lord's Table. The early Christians used to have a meal together before the Lord's Supper. The rich people did not share their food with the slaves and other poor people. Some were even getting drunk at the Lord's Table. The Scriptures tell us that God was very angry with these people and he punished some of them because of their sin. We read, 'For this reason many are weak and sick among you, and many sleep [are dead]' (1 Corinthians 11:30).

Some sins have terrible consequences. The drunkard might stumble in front of a truck and be badly injured. The drug-user might catch some terrible disease using infected needles. The list is endless.

May we all learn from this story that God expects everyone to obey his commandments. If we disobey, God may well punish such people at once. All people are called to trust in the Lord Jesus Christ and glorify him by obeying all that God has commanded.

Activities

● ●

a. Have you ever hurt yourself while doing something wrong?
b. How does God punish sinners in this world?

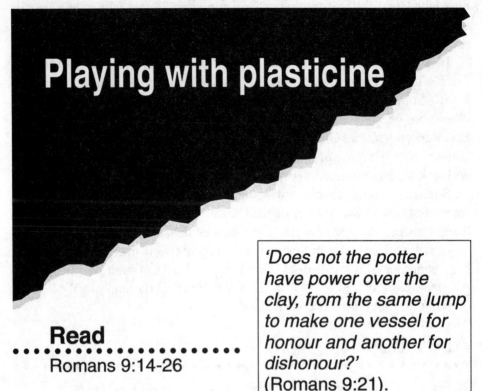

Playing with plasticine

Read
....
Romans 9:14-26

> 'Does not the potter have power over the clay, from the same lump to make one vessel for honour and another for dishonour?'
> (Romans 9:21).

When I was a schoolteacher, one of the craft lessons that the children always liked was working with plasticine or clay. With this the children could mould almost anything they wanted. Sometimes they would mould animals, sometimes the human head, sometimes ships — anything they wanted to make they would try.

In wintertime one of the problems with plasticine is that it can be quite hard — sometimes almost as hard as a stone. Before the children could begin any moulding it was necessary to make the plasticine soft. To do this you must start rubbing it about in your hands. Gradually the warmth from your hands will soften the plasticine. If you take a large lump it is almost impossible to work with and make soft.

The children who took large lumps of hard, cold plasticine found it necessary to tear or cut off a small piece — and make it nice and pliable. They would then take another piece and do the same with that. Some children would roll the plasticine on their wooden desks, stick their fingers into it and at times even punch their fist into the softening lump. As they worked on the lump, it became soft, making it possible to mould that once hard lump of plasticine into some shape they wanted.

Sometimes they were very happy with their moulding and kept it for a long time. But sometimes things just didn't go the way they wanted, so the plasticine was squashed up and thrown into a tin to be used another time.

Every time the children worked with the plasticine I was reminded of our text which tells us that God is like a potter who works with clay. God wants to mould his people to become something very special. In the book of Romans Paul writes about Christians who were to be 'conformed to the image of His Son' (Romans 8:29). When God sends his Holy Spirit into anyone's heart, that person becomes a new creature in Christ. All of God's people are part of his family. Christians are sons and daughters of the living God. This means we must be made into people who resemble the Lord Jesus Christ, who is our elder Brother.

As we read the Bible we find out what we must do to please God. We find his laws that must be obeyed. Remember that Jesus said, 'If you love Me, keep My commandments' (John 14:15). We shall find it a great pleasure to show our love of Christ by obedience to God's law.

If we say we are Christians, others will know this to be true when we act like the Lord Jesus Christ. We will, by his grace, love God with all our hearts and minds and souls. We will honour Jesus above all else. We will thank God for placing his Holy Spirit in our souls. And we will love one another just as Christ loved us. We will not hurt anyone and when we sin we will be truly repentant and ask God to forgive us. God has made a special promise to his people when they fall into sin: 'If we confess our sins, He is faithful and just to forgive us our sins and to cleanse us from all unrighteousness' (1 John 1:9).

Every day you should pray that God will mould you into the likeness of his Son Jesus Christ. But sometimes we are stubborn and we don't want to change. We still like some of our sins. But God will change us, for he is the all-powerful and loving Potter. Just as the children had to thump and smash the plasticine to make it soft, in order to mould it the way they wanted, God also sometimes has to be hard with you to make you soft so that the Holy Spirit can mould you.

Sometimes God is forced to discipline his people to bring about changes. The writer to the Hebrews says, 'For whom the Lord loves He chastens...' (Hebrews 12:6) and, 'Now no chastening seems to be joyful for the present, but grievous; nevertheless, afterward it yields the peaceable fruit of right-eousness to those who have been trained by it' (Hebrews 12:11).

Just as your Mum and Dad train you to be good family members, so then God trains his people to be great citizens of the kingdom of heaven.

Activities

a. Name something you have moulded. Did it really look as it should have done?
b. With some plasticine try moulding a face.
c. In what way does God mould his people?
d. Who is God moulding his people to be like?

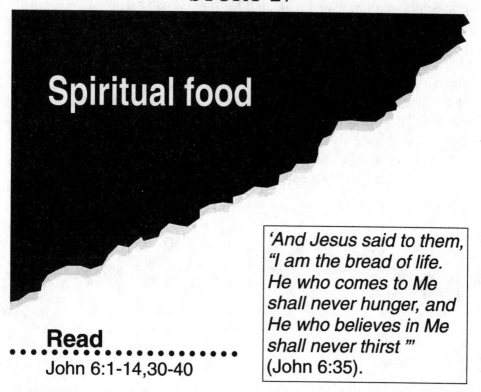

Spiritual food

'And Jesus said to them, "I am the bread of life. He who comes to Me shall never hunger, and He who believes in Me shall never thirst "' (John 6:35).

Read
John 6:1-14,30-40

I'm sure that all of us enjoy our foods, or at least most foods. I know that some young people don't like eating their vegetables, but most of the time we enjoy what is prepared for our meals. We all know that if we do not eat we will die. Daily we need energy to do what we want to do. I remember when I was attending high school and played football, my mother used to pack me some brown sugar sandwiches which I was to eat before the game started. I enjoyed these sweet sandwiches, but also knew that the sugar would give me extra energy for the game.

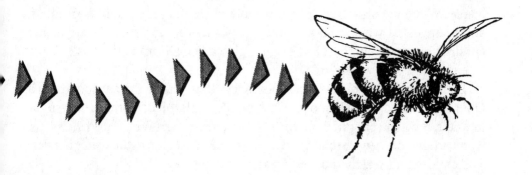

As we grow older we eat different types of food. I have two new grandchildren, Simon and Kim, and for some months they just drank their mother's milk. But now they eat anything they can get their hands on. Soon they will be sitting down and eating a piece of steak!

Every part of God's creation needs food to survive. I would like to tell you about a very interesting creature — a bee. There are times when you are out in the garden that you will see the bees at work gathering pollen from the flowers. They take the pollen back to their hives and there it is made into honey. But the bee also pollinates the flowers, so seeds are formed and the next generation of plants come.

At school one day, one of the girls in my class came to me with a bee in her handkerchief. All the bee could do was crawl very slowly. Samantha asked me, 'Sir, what is wrong with this bee? It can't fly. It was crawling around on the ground so I just picked it up. Is it dying?'

Well, that bee was dying and it could not fly at all. It had simply run out of energy. Apparently a bee is fed enough energy when it leaves the hive to fly to and back from the flowers where the pollen is. Sometimes the bee does not have enough energy to get back to the hive, so it falls to the ground and dies. Bees can be sometimes caught out when a wind begins to blow and they find they need more energy than they expected to return home.

As it was time for the class to return after lunch, I asked Samantha to put the bee in a bottle and said we would try an experiment when everyone came inside. When the class had settled we talked about the bee and its problem and I suggested we should give the bee something to drink. Some of the children began to laugh. 'How do you give a bee a drink?' they asked.

I replied, 'Just watch this!'

I put the bee on a piece of cardboard and then placed the cardboard on a table out in the open. Then one of the children dissolved some white sugar in water. It was a very good mixture of sugar and water. We poured the sweet water around the bee, so that wherever it waddled it came to the water barrier. The children all watched to see what would happen.

Within a few minutes the bee had come to the water and we could all see it poking its face into the sugary mixture. Some children could even see it poke out its mouth and suck up the sweet water. The bee did this for ten or twenty seconds and then just stood there doing nothing. The children were very quiet as they waited and watched.

A couple of minutes later the bee began to slowly move its wings. Then the wings began to move very quickly. Finally the bee flew up into the air, and I guess, headed back to its hive. All of the children began to clap and cheer. It was really good to see that tiny bee off on its way home. If you find a bee on the grass in your garden, you might like to try the same experiment.

We need food to keep our bodies going, but we should always remember that we are not all body. We have something very precious within our bodies — that is, our souls. And just as our bodies need food to grow, so also do our souls. However, I'm sure that my soul will not survive on a diet of bacon and eggs with some chocolate. Our souls need spiritual food in order to grow, and that food is Christ. Our text tells us that Jesus Christ is the bread of life. If we feast spiritually upon him our souls will grow and we shall become fine Christian folk.

The apostle Paul was a great missionary, but he knew that he was a weak man. Many were the difficulties he faced as he travelled about preaching and teaching. In his own strength he knew he could achieve nothing of lasting value for his Lord. But he wrote some very precious words that are of great comfort to all of God's people. Paul was locked up in a Roman prison. To most people it appeared as if Paul could not serve the Lord while he was chained up, but he wrote to the Christians at Philippi and said, 'I can do all things through Christ who strengthens me' (Philippians 4:13).

All Christians know that they are weak, and to carry out their Christian duties must depend upon energy from Christ. It is in the weakness of his people that Christ does great things. This then brings glory to Christ. In fact the Lord Jesus said to Paul, 'My grace is sufficient for you, for My strength is made perfect in weakness.' So Paul could then say, 'Therefore most gladly I will rather boast in my infirmities, that the power of Christ may rest upon me' (2 Corinthians 12:9).

How is it, then, that we can feast our souls upon Christ, who is our spiritual bread from heaven? How is it that we are able to grow spiritually?

There are many ways, but most important of all is to open our Bibles and read what God has to say to us. In Psalm 19:10, King David says that the Word of God was sweeter to him than honey from the honeycomb. Then we read in Psalm 119:103 these precious words: 'How sweet are Your words to my taste, sweeter than honey to my mouth!'

As we read the Bible we learn what God would have us do — God speaks to us through his Word and as we begin to live the Christian life our souls grow. We also need to be taught the things of God, and this means that we attend Sunday school, if such is available. But most important of all we must attend worship, where with other Christians we praise and glorify God for his goodness to us. There we also learn more and more about our God and our salvation in Christ. And when Christ's people come together to sit at the Lord's Table for the communion service, there they are strengthened in their faith. At the Lord's Supper, Christians think particularly about God's great love towards them, as it is seen in the life and death of the Lord Jesus Christ.

We need to mix more and more with other Christians. This will help us grow spiritually. We need to read good books that teach us about God and his glory. There are so many good books about today! Get some of these books and read them. And if you are blessed by reading a good spiritual book, tell others about it — or even buy a copy and give it away. This is a means by which we can witness to the love of Christ in our hearts.

And pray. Each day talk to God. That is what prayer is. It is telling God how much you love him. It is thanking God for what he has done for you. It is praising God. And prayer is asking God to help you in your spiritual life. All of these things will strengthen your soul and make it grow.

When the apostle Paul wrote to the Corinthians he told some of them that they were still babies in Christ. He said, 'I fed you with milk and not with solid food' (1 Corinthians 3:2). The writer to the Hebrews told some people that they were still spiritual babies and were not growing in their faith. We read, 'For though by this time you ought to be teachers, you need someone to teach you ... you have come to need milk and not solid food. For everyone who partakes only of milk is unskilled in the word of righteousness, for he is a babe. But solid food belongs to those who are mature, that is, those who by reason of use have their senses exercised to discern both good and evil' (Hebrews 5:12-14).

Christian, use all the means that are available to grow in Christ — to grow up to be a mature Christian, even though you may still be young in years.

May God, through his Holy Spirit, cause you all to grow up to be fine Christians.

Activities

a. Why do humans eat food and what foods should we eat?
b. What food does God give us to keep us alive spiritually?
c. Try to find a bee that has run out of energy. Help it to get going again.

Bogged down in the front lawn

Read
Genesis 37:1-22
and 45:1-15

'And we know that all things work together for good to those who love God, to those who are the called according to His purpose' (Romans 8:28).

These words are among the most comforting that we find in the whole of Scripture. They are words of encouragement when everything about us seems to be falling apart. They remind Christians that all the events that take place are for their good. Even when things go terribly wrong in our lives, God is using those very incidents to bring glory to his name and to benefit his people.

Our reading for today is about a young man named Joseph who was hated by his brothers. They sold Joseph into slavery. You can read of all his troubles. But God had a very special purpose in all that happened to Joseph.

When Joseph met his wicked

brothers they were terrified that he might put them to death. But Joseph said to them, 'But now, do not therefore be grieved or angry with yourselves because you sold me here: for God sent me before you to preserve life... So it was not you who sent me here, but God' (Genesis 45:5,8).

Of course this is hard to believe at times, but let us remember that God is all-powerful and always does as he purposes. We read in Daniel 4:35: 'He [God] does according to His will in the army of heaven and among the inhabitants of the earth. No one can restrain His hand or say to Him, "What have You done?"' Everything God does is for the good of his people and for his own glory!

Some years ago I told my wife I would preach on our text for this story. I had spent some time in my study, when my wife knocked on the closed door and came in. She said, 'Jim, I want you to come to the front door and see something.'

Our home at that time was the church manse, hidden behind the church building. Between the manse and the highway we had a nice lawn, and I always tried to keep it well cut and tidy. On this particular day it had been raining quite a lot and the ground was very soft. My wife took me to the front door, quietly opened it and pointed to the front lawn. There to my horror I saw a car bogged down on the lawn in front of the church building. I couldn't believe my eyes. I looked at my wife and asked, 'How could such a thing happen? No one would park on someone's front lawn like that. Who did it? Where is the person?'

My wife quietly answered, 'A lady has just been up and told me what happened. She had to go next door to the doctor's surgery and as there was no parking place on the roadside, she decided she'd park on the church lawn.' 'But,' I replied, 'No one could be that silly. Just look at the lawn! Wait till she comes back!'

With that I walked down the steps and over to the car. It was bogged up to the axle. I was really furious with what had happened, so I set off back to the house. On the way, as I was passing the wood heap, I grabbed the axe and began to chop some wood. I thought that would help me get over the shock, but — would you believe it? — the axe handle broke!

I walked up to my wife, who was still standing on the verandah, watching her angry husband, and said, 'When that lady returns I will have something to say to her!'

My wife Valerie then said to me (she knew my sermon text for that Sunday morning service), 'Jim, remember, "And we know that all things work together for good to those who love God, to those who are the called according to His purpose."'

I felt rebuked and went into the study to work on my sermon. I knew that the lady would return, because she would need help to get her car out. I began to think about the incident and wondered why God had caused such a thing to happen. The lawn in that spot had been ruined, but I knew that it could easily be fixed.

'Well,' I thought to myself, 'I will have a perfect opportunity to speak to that lady about Christ. She can't get away from me and I'm sure she will listen because she knows the trouble she has caused.'

When the lady returned from the doctor she was very apologetic. Over and over again she said how sorry she was. She said she had been running late for the doctor's appointment and the front lawn of the church seemed just the best place to park. I then told her who I was and asked her if she attended church anywhere. She said she didn't and so I spoke to her about Christ and was able to give her a small booklet about the Christian life. I'm sure she was amazed that I was not angry with her. I invited her to worship, but I never saw her again.

Often I wonder why God sent that woman in a car, to get bogged down on the church lawn. But this I know: that God had a special purpose. Maybe God was teaching me a lesson — to believe and practise what I was preaching about. Or could it have been that the opportunity given me to speak to the lady about Jesus was a step in her coming to saving faith in Christ? It may well be that on the Judgement Day I will meet that lady again as we together sing the praises of our loving Lord and Saviour Jesus Christ.

When I got behind her car to push while she drove, the wheels spun around so fast that mud was thrown all over me. At least I now know where to stand when pushing a car out of a bog!

Activities

● ●

a. What unpleasant thing has happened to you lately?
b. In what way has it helped you become a better person?

A cry for help

Read
• •
Daniel 3

> 'Call upon Me in the day
> of trouble; I will deliver
> you, and you shall
> glorify Me'
> (Psalm 50:15).

In the Bible we find many promises made by God. We read, 'Believe on the Lord Jesus Christ, and you will be saved...' (Acts 16:31). This is a very precious promise that Jesus will ensure comes to pass. We also read the words of our God: 'I will never leave you nor forsake you' (Hebrews 13:5). This promise is found in the Old Testament as well as the New. It means that no matter where we are, no matter what difficulties we face, our God will be with us and he will never leave us. Our text also contains a very special promise: 'Call upon Me in the day of trouble; I will deliver you...'

I would like to tell you another story about Smokey. As you know, he was always getting himself into trouble. Usually when we returned from school, the girls called out to Smokey. They liked to give him a big hug when they arrived home each day. He would rub himself around their legs, and look up into their eyes, knowing that someone would pick him up and give him a cuddle. He also knew that they would go to the refrigerator and get him something to eat. In fact most of the time he would run to the refrigerator to remind them that he was hungry.

One day after school Smokey did not come when he was called. At first the girls did not worry as they thought he might be out visiting another cat. But as the time went by Smokey still did not come home. He was nowhere to be found. We called and called, but Smokey just didn't appear.

111

That night the girls went to bed quite unhappy. They thought the worst. Maybe Smokey had been bitten by a snake. Maybe he had been hit by a car and had crawled away to die. Maybe he was badly hurt. But as they went to bed, they asked me to call them early in the morning so they could look for the lost cat.

Morning came and when the girls called out to Smokey there was still no reply. It looked as if Smokey was gone this time. The girls said that when they came home from school that day they would really search for their pet cat.

That afternoon we quickly came home from school to find out that Smokey had not returned. We all wondered, 'Where can he be?' I felt sure that Smokey was dead. He had never been away for so long. The girls changed their clothes and began to call out, 'Here Smokey! Smokey!' They looked about the garage and in the bushes around the house fence, but no Smokey was to be found. Then they began to look under the house. Now, there was not much space under the house. A cat could crawl in there, but it would be difficult for a human to get under the low flooring.

Suddenly Lisa called out, 'I can hear him! I can hear Smokey meowing! Dad, come quickly! He's under the house! He must be sick!'

We all got down on our hands and knees and looked into the darkness under the house. We began to call out Smokey's name. Then we listened. We heard a faint 'meow', but it seemed to be coming from miles away.

'Get the torch,' Cathie called out. 'His eyes will shine in the light.' But even though we could hear the faint 'meow', we couldn't see Smokey. The girls were becoming very upset.

'You'll have to crawl under the house, Dad,' they said. I didn't want to crawl under the house. I thought of all the spiders just waiting to bite anyone who came their way. So I said to the girls, 'I don't think he's under the house. He sounds a long way away.' For some reason I put my ear close to the ground and every time Smokey cried out for help, for that was what he was doing, it seemed as if his cry came from under the ground. Now I knew that Smokey always seemed to get himself into trouble, but I thought that he surely couldn't be underground.

So the girls called their mother out and said, 'Mum, you listen and tell us where you think Smokey is.' Poor Mum had to get down on her hands and knees and look under the house and listen. Then there came a 'meow'.

'I don't believe it,' my wife replied, 'but I think the sound is coming from under the ground, and it's not far away.'

Well, we all put our ears to the ground, listened and moved closer and closer to the place from which the meow came. Soon we were at a downpipe that was attached to the guttering around the house. When it rained the rainwater would run down a tin pipe into underground pipes and then flow out into the gutter beside the road.

I began to wonder, 'Would it be possible for that silly cat to somehow get into the pipe at the roadside and crawl along it as far as he could go?' It just had to be the answer.

So out came the spade and I began to dig down till I came to some earthenware pipes about half a metre underground. Smokey's 'meow' sounded a lot closer. Then I had to take a hammer and chisel and break the pipe open. As soon as I knocked the first small hole in the pipe I was sure I could see a cat's nose. With a few more blows the hole was big enough to see that it was Smokey. The girls were so happy to know that he was soon to be set free. My wife just stood there with an amazed look on her face and said, 'That stupid cat! He certainly gets himself into awkward spots!'

Soon Smokey was free. He had spent almost two days underground in a pipe into which he could hardly fit. He must have been playing on the roadside and then chased something up the pipe — or maybe he just wanted to see where the pipe took him. The further up the pipe he went, the darker it became. The pipe was so small he couldn't turn around. He just kept going till he could go no further. When he realized he was in real trouble, he cried out for help and waited. He was very fortunate that his cries for help were heard and that eventually he was rescued.

Christians suffer in this world as do all other people. Christians get sick and die. Christians experience happiness and sadness. In our lives we find that there are many times when we are in danger and need help. Sometimes we are in bodily danger and we cry out for help. Sometimes our faith in Jesus weakens and we fear that we are not Christians at all. In all of our troubles, we are commanded to cry to God for help. And the greatest wonder of all is that God hears our cries and he will come to our rescue.

God has not promised to save us from trouble and heartache, but has certainly promised to sustain us in our difficulties and by his grace we will pull through all that happens to us. We must always remember that our troubles can be testing times when we can show the people around us, and also ourselves, that we are Christians. At other times God uses trials and difficulties to make us better Christians, because we have to depend more and more on Jesus for help and comfort.

In such times, the advice of the apostle Paul is: 'Be anxious for nothing, but in everything by prayer and supplication, with thanksgiving, let your requests be made known to God; and the peace of God, which surpasses all understanding, will guard your hearts and minds through Christ Jesus' (Philippians 4:6-7).

Sometimes God rescues his people by removing them from this world to be with Christ in the home which he has prepared for them. He has promised that we shall never suffer beyond that which we can stand, for he has promised that his grace will be sufficient in all the circumstances of life.

When trouble comes, always tell the Lord Jesus what has happened, and seek his comfort and guidance. Read your Bibles, for it is through his Word that God guides and comforts his people.

Activities

● ●

a. How have you helped someone in need?
b. How does God help sinners?

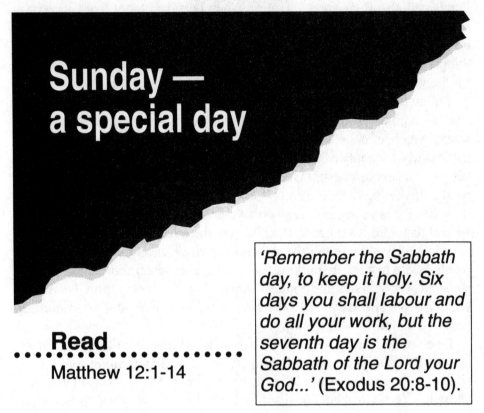

Sunday —
a special day

Read
Matthew 12:1-14

> *'Remember the Sabbath day, to keep it holy. Six days you shall labour and do all your work, but the seventh day is the Sabbath of the Lord your God...'* (Exodus 20:8-10).

This commandment, given to God's people the Jews, was important, for it reminded the people of two very important events. First of all, it reminded the people that God created the world in six days, and that God rested from the work of creation on the seventh day (Genesis 2:1-3; Exodus 20:11).

However, in Deuteronomy 5:15 we read a second reason given to the people of Israel for keeping the Sabbath day as a special day: 'And remember that you were a slave in the land of Egypt, and that the Lord your God brought you out from there by a mighty hand and by an outstretched arm; therefore the Lord your God commanded you to keep the Sabbath day.'

On the Sabbath day, God's people of Israel remembered God creating all things and also their great salvation when he saved them from slavery in Egypt and led them to the land of Canaan, which would be their home. It was a very special day for the Jewish people — a time for remembering great things, as well as a day for the resting of their bodies, so they would be ready for the week's work that lay before them.

Following the death of the Lord Jesus Christ, God's people, who came from all nations, began to meet together for worship on the first day of the week, which is called 'the Lord's Day'. This is the day when we can particularly remember the resurrection of our Saviour. It is the day when Christians meet to worship God and glorify the Lord Jesus. It is a day when most churches have their Sunday schools for young folk.

When I was young and lived on my parents' farm, Sunday was always a special day. The cows had to be milked in the morning, and then we would attend Sunday school and the worship service. During the afternoon, we would have a rest before milking the cows again. Sometimes we would visit someone who was sick and couldn't get out. We didn't play sport, but the day was used in a special way for the glory of God. Having our afternoon rest prepared us for the week's work.

One Sunday, when we were all having a rest before milking the cows, I lay on my bed thinking about fishing. It was a lovely afternoon, and I really wanted to go and throw a line in the river. I knew Mum and Dad wouldn't be happy if I did this, but I decided to climb out of the bedroom window and soon I was down at the riverbank, line in the water and waiting for a fish to bite.

Suddenly I had a great tug on my line and after some pulling I had a big mud crab up on the river bank. It was a huge crab with nippers snapping at everything that came near it. The crab had become tangled in my fishing line and so it couldn't escape. After some trouble I had it in a bag. But in the midst of my excitement I had a terrible thought. I was supposed to be lying down and having a rest. I knew Mum and Dad would not be happy about my fishing trip, but I had a crab that was so big it would be a feed for the family. What could I do? If I took it home I would be in trouble for using the Lord's Day in a way that was not pleasing to my parents. If I didn't take it home, no one would ever know about my tremendous catch.

Eventually I decided to take the crab home. I had to show it to my parents and brother. I knew I would be in trouble. When I arrived home I woke up Mum and Dad and showed them my catch. They weren't very happy with me, but we had the crab for tea. It was delicious.

Now that I'm older I love the Lord's Day greatly. It is the day when I am able to meet with the saints — all those people who are born again — and together worship our gracious God.

I don't always have a rest on the Lord's Day, because I can now rest any day. In fact I now find it better to rest on Saturday, so that I am wide awake and better refreshed to worship God on Sunday.

When Jesus was on earth he set us an example for the way we should spend the Christian Sabbath — the Lord's Day. He used the day for worship, healing the sick and doing good. He told his listeners what God expected of his people on the Sabbath day. Jesus met a sick man and asked a question of the Pharisees and lawyers who were with him: 'Is it lawful to heal on the Sabbath?'

Those to whom Jesus spoke said nothing, so Christ healed the man, and then said, 'Which of you, having a donkey or an ox that has fallen into a pit, will not immediately pull him out on the Sabbath day?' (Luke 14:3-5).

I find Sunday a wonderful day to visit elderly people and people who are sick. Sunday is a great day to spend time reading some of my books about God and his salvation in Jesus Christ. I even use time on Sunday to write to my Christian friends and others, to give them the news and to tell them of the great things God has done for me. I try to make the Lord's Day a very important day. It is never an unhappy day, but a day to serve and worship the Lord in a very special way.

Because the people of the world generally care nothing for God, and treat Sunday as they do every day, Christians should show the world that we are different. We should let the world know that Christ is precious to us and that we can honour our God by keeping the Lord's Day holy.

Activities

● ●

a. What is the most exciting day of the year for you?
b. Why is Sunday a special day?
c. What can you do to make Sunday a special day?

Obey your parents

Read
Luke 2:41-52

'Children, obey your parents in the Lord, for this is right. "Honour your father and mother," which is the first commandment with promise: "that it may be well with you and you may live long on the earth." And you, fathers, do not provoke your children to wrath, but bring them up in the training and admonition of the Lord' (Ephesians 6:1-4).

One of the greatest ways to show our parents that we love and honour them is by obeying them. Of course, if our parents ask us to do something which means breaking God's law, then we must respectfully say, 'No. I will always obey God first.'

This, of course, doesn't happen very often in the lives of most young people. Parents see dangers that their children don't see. Parents are usually wiser than their children. And parents want the very best for their children. That is why they teach you about the things of God and his Son Jesus Christ. That is why they take you to worship and Sunday school. That is why they provide good food for your body. And of course, that is why they encourage you to do the best you can in your school studies.

Mum and Dad so often see danger where children think they are quite safe. I have a friend who has a wooden leg below the knee. When we were at school he used to play cricket. Occasionally the ball would hit him on his wooden leg and knock it out from under him. He would fall flat on his face. When we attended high school, I remember him one morning arriving late. He had a motor bike and when he arrived at school it looked as if he had had an accident. When the teacher asked him what had happened Joshua replied: 'Sir, I had an accident on my bike and knocked my leg off.' Everyone laughed.

When Joshua was a young boy he lived near the railway tracks. He always enjoyed getting down to that area, where he played with his friends on the railway trucks. Joshua's Mum and Dad didn't like him playing on the railway lines and warned him many times that he was not to go and play there. But like many young people, Joshua thought that he knew best.

One day he went off to the railway yard with his friends. Some of the boys with him began to push a heavy coal wagon along the tracks. Joshua was having a great time.

Suddenly he slipped. The moving wagon ran over his leg and cut it off just below the knee. Poor young Joshua very nearly lost his life.

God tells you that you are to 'obey your parents in the Lord'. This means that you honour God by obeying your parents. We also find that there is a general promise made by God to those who obey their parents — a long and happy life.

May you all respect, love and obey your parents as you would the Lord Jesus Christ. Many young people today are rude to their parents and cause their parents much heartache.

A friend sent me the following cutting out of a newspaper.

O.K. IN THE END

'Despairing Dads, don't worry. It turns out right in the end according to a homily popping up on a few fridge doors. But first Dad has to go through several stages in the eyes of his offspring.

AGE 4

'My Dad can do anything!'

AGE 7

'Dad knows a lot, a whole lot.'

AGE 12

'Dad doesn't quite know everything.'

AGE 15

'Oh well, naturally Dad doesn't understand.'

AGE 21

'My father? Hopelessly old-fashioned and out of date!'

AGE 25

'He has a good idea now and again.'

AGE 35

'I must find out what Dad thinks about this.'

AGE 50

'I wish I could talk it over with Dad.'

Jesus grew up in a family and set an example for all children to follow. If you have read the passage of Scripture set for you at the commencement of this lesson, you will have read in verse 51 that Jesus was 'subject [obedient]' to Mary and Joseph.

The Bible also has something to say to Dads and parents generally. Parents are not to irritate their children and cause them heartache. Parents are to respect their children, ensuring they have a joyful and secure family life in which they are always treated fairly.

Let us do all we can to make sure our family has a happy, spiritual home, where Christ is Lord and Saviour of each member.

Activities

a. Make a list of the people we should obey when they tell us what we should do?

b. Why should you obey your parents?

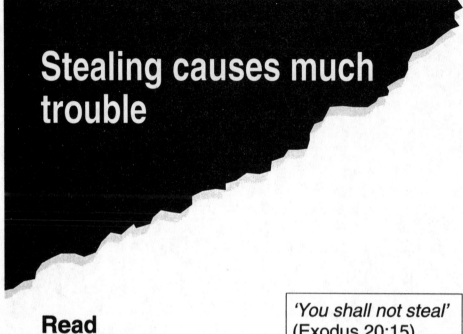

Stealing causes much trouble

Read
....
Malachi 3:8-12
and Acts 5:1-11

'You shall not steal'
(Exodus 20:15).

God has given us many things to enjoy. Most people have many possessions which they call their own. I'm sure that the readers of this book own many things that they treasure. In our world there are things that belong to us. We might lend them to someone else, but we always expect them to be returned.

Sometimes people break into homes and steal the possessions of others. Our house has been broken into several times. It is very upsetting to come home and find things that were treasured have been stolen. It should make us realize that the things of this world do not last.

What is really important is that we have treasure in heaven, for we know that that treasure can never be stolen. Our greatest treasure in heaven is Jesus Christ in whom we have faith. Also, the righteousness of Christ is put to our account. Then there are the works of righteousness, done in the name of Christ. The Lord has a record of our faithfulness and even though we do not deserve rewards for doing what we should do, God will reward us beyond anything we could ever imagine.

One afternoon as the classes were leaving school the librarian came to me and said, 'Jim, a radio is missing from the library. It was there just before the class was dismissed, but now it is gone. I think it's been stolen.'

It was too late to do anything that afternoon, but the next morning at the school assembly I asked for the radio to be returned. The children were told that the theft would have to be reported to the police. This was necessary in order for the replacement to be claimed from the insurance company. I told the children that stealing was a wicked thing to do, but if the person returned the radio, the police need not be informed. But the radio was not returned, and after a week or so the theft was reported. Eventually a new radio was purchased for the library.

It was very disappointing to know that among the schoolchildren there was a thief — a person who could not be trusted. We must remember that stealing hurts the person who has had his or her property stolen, but even worse than that, stealing is a sin against God, because God has said, 'You shall not steal' (Exodus 20:15).

The matter was soon forgotten and it seemed as if the thief would never be caught. But about six months later, a girl came to me and said, 'Sir, do you remember the radio that was stolen from the library? I know who stole it.' I was amazed and asked who the person was and how she found out. The answer was very simple: 'Sir, I heard him telling another boy.'

I soon had the suspected thief in the office and said, 'I believe it was you who stole the library radio six months ago. Is this true?'

The boy, who was about ten years of age, began to look down at the floor. He said, with tears beginning to form in his eyes, 'Yes, sir, I stole the radio.'

He told me that he had seen the radio and decided to steal it. He had a radio at home and didn't need the one he had taken. He had put it in his school bag and taken it home. But then he didn't know what to do with it. He knew that if his mother or father or even his brothers or sisters saw it, they would ask questions and he would be in real trouble. Eventually he hid the radio in the very bottom of his cupboard. He couldn't use what he had stolen and for six months he had felt very guilty. Then he decided he had to tell a friend what he had done. And as he was confessing his secret to his friend, the girl overheard his words.

The boy was so sorry for what he had done. Tears flowed from his eyes and he asked, 'Sir, do you have to tell Mum and Dad?'

Now there are some sins, while terrible in the sight of God, that are never known about by our friends. They are secret sins. But always remember that God knows all about us. Not only did I have to tell the boy's mother and father, but I had to tell the police also. Then the matter had to be reported to the insurance company that had replaced the stolen radio. That boy has grown up to be a very fine man, but he will always remember that foolish act of stealing.

The commandment says, 'You shall not steal!' (Exodus 20:15). The Bible tells us of the terrible results of stealing. Read the story of Achan who stole from the Lord. His sin brought great harm and shame upon the Israelites. Furthermore, he and his family were punished by death (Joshua 7).

We can steal in many ways. Some people are lazy workers and so get paid for work they do not do. These people steal from their boss. Some people steal from God by not supporting the work of the church, both with money and service which should be given. The reading in Malachi tells us that the Jewish people stole from God by not giving their tithe to the temple priests. God has given us so much. We owe him our everything. Stealing is a great sin. There are many people in jails who are thieves. No one likes a thief.

May we each one appreciate what God has given us. And if God has given us much of the things of this world, let us ever be ready to share what we own with others. Part of our Christian life is to do good to all people, especially other Christians and people who are in need.

Activities

a. What would you do if your best friend showed you something he had stolen from a schoolmate?
b. If you stole something what should you do?

A sheep in trouble

Read
Luke 10:25-37

'Therefore, as we have opportunity, let us do good to all, especially to those who are of the household of faith' (Galatians 6:10).

A grazier always looks after his cattle because they are his, and they are the means by which he makes a living. Sheep farmers have a difficult job looking after their sheep, as changes in the weather can result in many deaths, especially if the sheep have been shorn and the snow starts to fall.

In Australia there are dingoes that hunt the sheep and kill wherever they can. The farmer has to keep a careful watch on his animals to protect them from many dangers. If a sheep farmer was riding his horse through the bush and found one of his sheep caught in a blackberry vine, he would stop and carefully free it from its prickly jail. If the farmer found a neighbour's sheep in trouble, he would do all he could to rescue that sheep as well.

One day a sheep farmer was riding through some rough country, checking the property fences, when he heard a sheep bleating. He stopped his horse and listened. When he heard the cry again he could tell the direction from which it was coming.

Soon the farmer was standing at the top of a hole, at the bottom of which was a stranded sheep. The man knew that the sheep would die unless he did something. He also knew that the sheep did not belong to him, but that didn't matter. He simply saw a sheep that needed help. The hole was too deep to jump into and he didn't have any way to lift the sheep out. Suddenly he remembered the shovel he carried when he was checking the fences. He took it from the horse saddle and slowly and carefully began to fill the hole in which the sheep was stranded. As the hole was filled in the sheep kept moving up on the earth that was shovelled in.

After a time the sheep was nearing the ground level. The farmer was able to grab it by its wool and drag it to the top of the hole. The silly sheep was overjoyed and ran off into the bush looking for its mates. The farmer hopped on his horse, thankful that he had been able to save his neighbour's sheep.

That sheep farmer sets us an example that we should follow in our daily life. The apostle Paul tells us in our text that we are to do good to all people — and that 'all' means every human being, even our enemies.

Jesus told the story of 'the Good Samaritan' (Luke 10:25-37). The Jews didn't like the Samaritans and the Samaritans kept out of the way of the Jews. But in Christ's parable we are told of a Jew who was attacked by thieves and left for dead. Some Jewish folk came along the road, even a priest, and they gave no help to the injured man. But a Samaritan who came along helped the injured man to his donkey and even paid for him to spend time at an inn, while he recovered.

We are to show kindness to everyone, even those who hate us and treat us as their enemies.

The apostle Paul wrote in our text that we have a very special responsibility to our fellow Christians. We are truly brothers and sisters of all who trust in Jesus. Together, we make up the church which is the family of God. We have been adopted into God's family and Jesus Christ is our elder Brother. When we hear of a fellow Christian being in need, we must always help. But it doesn't stop there. We are to give help and do good to every person, especially our brothers and sisters in Christ.

The shepherd in our story was very interested in the well-being of his sheep, but he also gave help to his neighbour's sheep. We must do likewise. When we do good to our brothers and sisters in Christ, it is as if we do good to Jesus himself.

Jesus spoke of his second coming to earth and the judgement that would follow. He said, 'When the Son of Man comes in His glory, and all the holy angels with Him, then He will sit on the throne of His glory. All the nations will be gathered before Him, and He will separate them one from another, as a shepherd divides his sheep from the goats. And He will set the sheep on His right hand, but the goats on the left. Then the King will say to those on His right hand, "Come, you blessed of My Father, inherit the kingdom prepared for you from the foundation of the world: for I was hungry and you gave Me food; I was thirsty and you gave Me drink; I was a stranger and you took Me in; I was naked and you clothed Me; I was sick and you visited Me; I was in prison and you came to Me." Then the righteous will answer Him saying, "Lord, when did we see You hungry and feed You, or thirsty and give You drink? When did we see You a stranger and take You in, or naked and clothe You? Or when did we see You sick, or in prison, and come to You?" And the King will answer and say to them, "Assuredly, I say to you, inasmuch as you did it to one of the least of these My brethren, you did it to Me'" (Matthew 25:31-40).

May each one of you do good to all people; and those of my readers who are Christians, remember that you have a special responsibility to your brothers and sisters in Christ.

Activities

● ●

a. How have you helped other people?
b. Why did you help them?

I can still move quickly

Read
• • • • • • • • • • • • • • • • • • • •
Revelation 12:7-12

'Be sober, be vigilant;
because your adversary
the devil walks about like
a roaring lion, seeking
whom he may devour'
(1 Peter 5:8).

I'm sure that most of you are young and fit. You probably enjoy sport and move with great ease. But over the years I've found I can't always do the things I used to do. I find it hard to run for any distance, and I can't jump the fence like I once could. Years ago I could climb up a tree like a monkey, but now I can only remember what I once did. Sometimes even bending down is a problem. But when the unexpected happens I'm sure we can all move very fast.

Some time ago, a friend, Robert, and I had the job of clearing some rusty sheets of tin from a church paddock. We both grew up in the country and we knew that sometimes snakes found a sheet of tin was a good place to sleep under. It would become very warm in the sun and as snakes like warmth this was a delightful place for a snake to rest.

We drove our small truck into the churchyard and looked at the sheets of iron stacked in a neat pile. There were other sheets lying around the yard as well. We talked jokingly with each other about the possibility of finding a snake under a sheet, and decided to be very careful in everything we did.

First of all we thought it best to pick up the sheets lying about the yard. Very slowly and carefully I lifted one end of the tin while Robert, with a very large stick in his hand, looked under to see if there was a snake. But there were no snakes. Soon we had all the scattered sheets on the truck. We felt very pleased with ourselves. We were no longer afraid of finding snakes.

Then we backed the truck closer to the heap of sheets of tin and began the slow hard job of lifting them one by one onto the truck. The pile was in the shade of a tall tree and this made our work a little easier. We were feeling very weary, so every now and again stopped to have a drink of water. Then back to work we went. As we lifted each sheet we looked carefully to make sure there were no snakes.

We only had a couple more to lift and put on the truck when suddenly we received a terrible fright. We carefully lifted the second last sheet of tin and began to move towards the truck. There was no snake to be seen anywhere. I think we were both smiling because our work was almost over.

Slowly we began to lift it onto the truck when we heard a thud — there on the tin was a huge green snake. It had been up in the tree all the time and at that moment had fallen off a limb.

I don't know who moved the fastest. I just dropped my end and ran for my life. Robert did the same, but he ran in the opposite direction. But I think the snake moved quicker than both of us, because by the time we stopped running and returned to the truck we couldn't find any sign of it. Maybe it received the biggest fright of all!

The snake was a green tree snake and wouldn't hurt anyone — except maybe a frog or two, which they like for dinner. We finished loading the sheets of iron and were soon on our way to the dump, to get rid of the rubbish. But we were shaking for hours after that. Even now, when I start to walk under a tree I look upwards to check for tree snakes.

In the Bible we are told of Satan, who sinned against our holy God. He was cast out of heaven and then on the newly created earth tempted Adam and Eve to sin. When Satan appeared to Eve and Adam, he did so as a snake. What a terrible mess our world has become because of sin!

We are all warned in the Bible that Satan is angry, because Jesus Christ, through his life and death, has overcome his power. Satan is a defeated enemy as far as Christians are concerned. But he still wants to cause us to fall into sin.

So read the text for today very carefully. The apostle Peter tells us plainly that we must be on guard against Satan and his temptations. We cannot see him, but he is very real. He is like a roaring, angry lion, who is ever trying to cause people to fall into sin.

When Satan tempts you to sin against God, ask Jesus Christ to give you the strength to say, 'No!' Through the Holy Spirit we can resist Satan's temptations and so remain faithful to our wonderful Saviour.

May God be pleased to bless you and keep you safe from the evil one.

Activities

a. Why do you think Satan was cast out of heaven?
b. How was Satan's power on earth defeated?
c. Why is Satan called 'a roaring lion'?

My brother's keeper!

Read

Genesis 4:1-15

'Then the Lord said to Cain, "Where is Abel your brother?"And he said, "I do not know. Am I my brother's keeper?"' (Genesis 4:9).

I have one brother, John, and he and I are good friends. We see each other every now and again and enjoy each other's company. We have many things in common — we both love fishing and we both were once schoolteachers. Both of us became ministers of the gospel. But we live well over a thousand kilometres away from each other and only get together a couple of times each year.

One day, when we were young, I decided to go fishing in the river that was not far from the farm on which we lived. Even when I was young I loved to buy some prawns and try to catch a feed of fish. Once I caught a very large crab in the river, but I've already told you about that in an earlier story. There were always plenty of jew fish, perch, flathead and bream to be caught.

This particular afternoon I set out to go fishing by myself. It was a lovely day and I felt sure that I'd catch plenty. When I arrived at the river I unpacked my fishing gear and soon had my line out waiting for a bite.

It wasn't too long before I had several quite large fish flapping about beside me. I was really enjoying my afternoon alone. I hadn't bothered to tell my brother that I was going fishing. When he found out what I had done he was not very happy. He tracked me down and sneaked over to a tree that

131

was close to the fishing spot. Then he did something that should never be done to anyone who is fishing. He picked up some stones, and began to throw one at a time into the river where my line was.

At first I didn't know what was happening. I thought it might have been a fish jumping out of the water, for sometimes a mullet will do that. But soon I noticed the splash was near my fishing area. Suddenly I turned about and saw John in the act of throwing another stone. Quickly he jumped behind a tree, hoping I would not see him. He was angry that I had not asked him to come with me.

I called out to him: 'Don't do that! You'll scare the fish away. Go home and leave me alone!' But John just picked up another stone and threw it into the river.

I shouted at him again: 'If you do that once more I'll come and get you!' But sure enough another stone landed in the river.

Then I lost patience with my brother. He was spoiling my fishing. I picked up a large, hard lump of dirt and threw it at him. Now I'm not usually a good shot with stones, but this time my aim was perfect. The clod of dirt hit him on the side of the head.

He gave out a great yell and said, 'I'm going home to tell Mum and Dad what you did! You'll get into trouble when you get home!' Then, with tears running down his face and some blood dribbling from his temple, John ran home as fast as he could.

I knew that I really was going to be in trouble, so I began packing up my fishing gear. I didn't hurry as there was no real reason to get home very quickly. I knew that I had done the wrong thing and I was sure that coming home with several nice fish was not going to protect me from Dad and Mum's anger.

When I reached the front door of our home, I heard Dad say, 'Jim! Is that you? Get in here this moment!'

I entered the door with the fish out in front of me, hoping that they would save me from what I was sure would happen. I started to speak: 'Dad, John came over and threw stones in the river where I was fishing. He was scaring the fish away. He's to blame!' But I soon realized that my words meant very little. I knew that the fish I had caught wouldn't protect me from my father's anger. I could see him taking the belt from round his trousers!

I learned that I was to take care of my young brother and be patient with him at all times, even when he annoyed me.

John and I go fishing together now. We don't throw stones at one another and we don't throw stones into the river where we are fishing. In fact we bought a boat in which we could go out to sea and catch the really big ones. John and I care for each other very much. He is my only brother and I think he is great.

And what about you, reader? How do you treat your brothers and sisters? Do you look after them and show patience even when they annoy you?

Our text is part of the story of two brothers, the sons of Adam and Eve. They should have been kind to each other, but Cain was jealous of Abel. In fact he was so jealous of Abel, because God accepted his sacrifice, that he killed him, burying his body in the ground so that it could not be found. But God knew what had happened and asked, 'Where is Abel your brother?' (Genesis 4:9). God expected Cain to look after his brother, even though he may have been jealous of him.

Let us remember that God is patient with sinners. How often we offend God with our sins, and yet he spares us, and gives us time to repent and trust in Jesus. God is gracious to us, and we should also be gracious, not just to our brothers and sisters, but to all people, even our enemies.

Activities

● ●

a. How do you take care of those you love?
b. Why don't you hurt the people you love?
c. What can you do so you can get on better with other people?

Beware of snakes!

Read
2 Thessalonians 3:6-15

> 'Go to the ant, you sluggard! Consider her ways and be wise, which, having no captain, overseer or ruler, provides her supplies in the summer, and gathers her food in the harvest. How long will you slumber, O sluggard? When will you rise from your sleep?'
> (Proverbs 6:6-9).

The Scriptures command us to work for a living. Even before sin entered the world we read in the Bible that 'The Lord God took the man and put him in the garden of Eden to tend and keep it ' (Genesis 2:15). I'm sure this was not hard work for Adam for, before sin, God's creation was perfect in every way.

After sin entered the world, work became a real problem not only for Adam and Eve, but for all their descendants. We read the words of God to Adam and Eve following their sin: 'Cursed is the ground for your sake; in toil you shall eat of it all the days of your life. Both thorns and thistles it shall bring forth for you, and you shall eat the herb of the field. In the sweat of your face you shall eat bread till you return to the ground, for out of it you were taken; for dust you are, and to dust you shall return' (Genesis 3:17-19).

Men and women work to provide the necessities of life — for homes, for food and clothing. Paul tells us that we must provide for our families. We are told in 1 Timothy 5:8: 'But if anyone does not provide for his own, and especially for those of his household, he has denied the faith and is worse than an unbeliever.' He also tells us that if 'anyone will not work, neither shall he eat' (2 Thessalonians 3:10). Today there are many people who want to work, but cannot find a job. Paul is not speaking about these people. Rather Paul is saying that the lazy person who just does not want to work must go without. He must get up, find a job and provide for himself and his family.

One of my friends Don was a truck driver. He drove a big semi-trailer. Sometimes men had to help load and unload the material he was carrying.

One unusual thing about Don was that he loved snakes. Now, I don't like snakes. They frighten me and when I see a snake I get out of the way. However, Don was different. He used to pick up any snake he saw, even if it was a poisonous one. He would put the snake in a bag and take it home so he could look more closely at it. Some he kept in cages and some he let go in the bush.

Most of the men at Don's workplace enjoyed their work, but there was one man who always went to the toilet when there was a job to be done. He would turn up ten minutes later when the heavy work was finished. He was not a worker, but was plain lazy. The other workers were always complaining about their lazy mate. One day the men asked Don, 'How can we get Fred to do his job like the rest of us? We're fed up with his laziness!'

Don replied in a determined voice, 'Leave it to me!' That afternoon Don went out into the bush and caught a black snake and put it in a bag to take to work. He had a plan.

The next morning, when the men were called out to do some heavy lifting, Fred disappeared into the toilet. Don then said to his workmates, 'Just watch this!'

Quickly he opened the boot of his car and took the black snake out of the bag. With the snake in his hand he crept over to the toilet where Fred was having a rest. Then Don shoved the snake under the toilet door.

Almost at once there was a terrible howl of distress and fear coming from Fred's lips. Fred must have jumped up on the toilet seat to get away from the snake and then climbed over the toilet door to escape. Fred ran from the toilet area as fast as he could, while all of his workmates laughed and laughed.

Fred got the message and now when the men are called out to work, he is there with them all, doing his bit. But Fred is scared. He never found out who put the snake under the toilet door. Till this day he still keeps an eye out just in case another snake turns up. This is a humorous, but true story.

Reader, we were created to praise and glorify God, and we can honour God in the work that we do. The apostle Paul was not just a great missionary, but he made tents (Acts 18:3) in order to provide for his needs. Remember that the Lord Jesus himself grew up in a family where his earthly father Joseph was a carpenter (Matthew 13:55). We can well imagine Jesus working in the carpenter's shop with Joseph.

As Christians we are to do the works of God — the works of love, serving God and others. God will not forget the good deeds we do in his name.

Many who read this book will find that their work is to study at school. If that is so, then always do your very best, and be assured that work is one way to serve God and bring glory to Christ.

Activities

a. What work would you like to have when you leave school?
b. Why should people work?
c. What work did God give Adam to do?

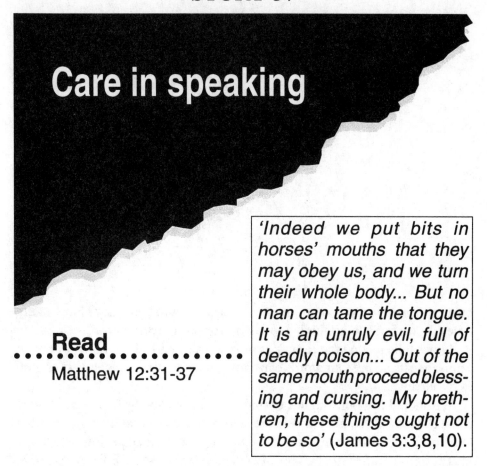

Care in speaking

Read
• • • • • • • • • • • • • • • • • • •
Matthew 12:31-37

'Indeed we put bits in horses' mouths that they may obey us, and we turn their whole body... But no man can tame the tongue. It is an unruly evil, full of deadly poison... Out of the same mouth proceed blessing and cursing. My brethren, these things ought not to be so' (James 3:3,8,10).

When I was much younger, I lived on a farm. This was a wonderful life. There was a lot of work to be done, but there also was much fun and games. We had a horse which we called 'Fred'. Now Fred was not the quietest horse in the district. When we went to catch him, he would sometimes put his head down, paw the ground and then race towards us. Usually then we dropped the bridle, ran for the closest fence and dived under. It was strange that Fred never did this to Dad, just to my brother and me.

However, after some time, we usually caught the horse and put on the bridle as well as the saddle. But Fred didn't like being told where to go. Many times he just galloped off where he wanted. It took so much strength to pull him up and turn him in the direction he had to go, that eventually a new bit had to be put in the bridle. The new bit was not a smooth one, but had a sharp edge so that when we pulled on the bridle he would come to a sudden halt. The bit hurt his mouth. But it was always difficult to control Fred.

The Bible tells us that our tongues are like that horse. They are hard to control. We all know that we say things that are hurtful to others, and how

many times do we say something we wish we could take back? How many times do we need to apologize to others for our hurtful words?

James tells us that the tongue is only a small part of the body, but what a nuisance it can be! Our words can cause so much harm to others — as well as to ourselves.

We should use our tongues to praise God and glorify Jesus Christ, who is the Saviour of his people. We are told in the Bible that the tongue is not to be used for 'filthiness, nor foolish talking, nor coarse jesting, which are not fitting, but rather [for] giving of thanks' (Ephesians 5:4). This means that we use our speech to encourage other Christians. We can use our words to witness to the love of God in our lives. Our tongues can be used to teach others of the good things of God.

This is what the apostle Paul teaches us in Ephesians 4:29: 'Let no corrupt communication proceed out of your mouth, but what is good for necessary edification, that it may impart grace to the hearers.'

We must use our tongues to glorify God, and we are not glorifying God when we gossip about other people. We are not to be tale-bearers. We are not to gossip about the sins of others. Paul told Titus to speak evil of no one (Titus 3:2). We are not to be involved in the rough talk and swearing that is so common today. We should pay close attention to what we watch and listen to on the television or radio. There are so many shows that are violent and contain coarse, godless language. No one should watch these programmes. They should be turned off as soon as you realize how vile they are.

In Psalm 34:13 King David tells us, 'Keep your tongue from evil, and your lips from speaking guile.' Let us all keep a close watch on our tongues, for Christ said, 'But I say to you that for every idle word that men may speak,

138

they will give account of it in the day of judgement. For by your words you will be justified, and by your words you will be condemned' (Matthew 12:36-37).

Let us ever use our tongues for the praise of God, and not for sin.

Activities

● ●

a. Have you ever said something that hurt a person?
b. How did you put things right with the person?

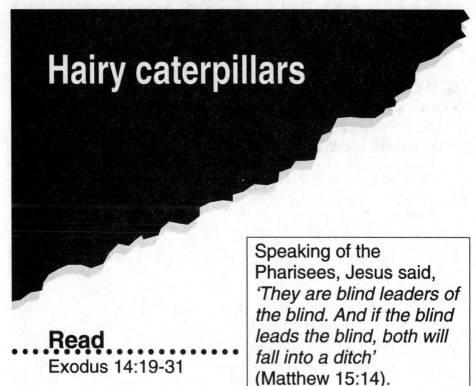

Hairy caterpillars

Read
Exodus 14:19-31

Speaking of the Pharisees, Jesus said, *'They are blind leaders of the blind. And if the blind leads the blind, both will fall into a ditch'* (Matthew 15:14).

The Pharisees were most certainly among the most religious people in Israel in the days when the Lord Jesus walked the earth. The Israelites looked up to the Pharisees because they believed that God loved them in a very special way. After all, weren't the Pharisees the religious leaders who always tried to obey the laws of God? They had also made laws, which they thought God would approve of. Then they obeyed their man-made laws as if they had the authority of God. They had the idea that God would love them because they did the very best they could to obey all the commandments.

The ordinary Jew also loved the Pharisees because they stood up to the Romans who had invaded Israel. The Pharisees, in particular, wanted to see the Roman armies out of Israel. Because the Pharisees were so respected

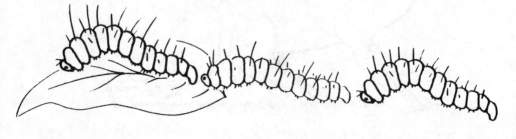

among the citizens of Israel, it is easy to understand why the people wanted to follow them.

The Lord Jesus warned the people of Israel that the Pharisees were blind in spiritual matters. They could see with their eyes, but they didn't understand the way of salvation. They were blind to spiritual truth.

We know that our 'good' deeds will not save us. The Bible tells us that 'There is none righteous, no, not one... There is none who does good, no, not one' (Romans 3:10,12).

There are people today who are also blind to spiritual truth, and tell us that if we do our best to obey God's law, then God will love us enough to take us to heaven when we die. And many people believe these lies. If they do not repent and trust in the works of Jesus alone for their salvation, they will be cast into hell.

The Pharisees and their followers remind me of some hairy grubs, or caterpillars, I once saw. There must have been thirty or so, all walking along, one after the other. Each caterpillar was touching the one in front and blindly following the leader. I don't know where they were going, and I wondered if even the leader itself knew. I thought they were silly creatures and called my wife and children to have a look at them.

Then I said, 'I wonder what would happen if we gradually moved the leader around so that he was touching the caterpillar who was last in line? I wonder if they would just follow each other around in a circle?'

So, very carefully, I moved the line of hairy caterpillars around so that the leader touched the one last in line. Then we stood back and watched.

Sure enough they just marched around in a circle. They looked like a line of very stupid creatures. We decided to leave them alone for an hour or so to see what would happen. An hour later they were still at it, walking around in a circle, each following the one in front. I think if we had left them that way, they would have walked and walked and eventually died from starvation. We broke up their line and once again there was a leader and off they went across the garden. They all seemed happy following their leader.

We must be very careful whom we follow. The apostle Paul was a great Christian leader who, following his conversion to Christ, faithfully followed Christ and his teachings. Paul said to the Corinthian Christians, 'Imitate me, just as I also imitate Christ' (1 Corinthians 11:1).

Humans are good at imitating everyone except the Lord Jesus. When my grandson Simon was just learning to crawl, I spent some time teaching him how to cough. He thought it was great fun. I would cough at him and he would cough at me. He imitated me!

In another story I told you that God is the great 'Potter' who, by his Holy Spirit, is moulding us into the likeness of Christ. We have a part to play in that process. We must read the Word of God and then live as Christ would have us to live. As we imitate Christ in our lives, because of God's Spirit within us, we will live lives pleasing to our heavenly Father.

In the reading for this lesson you will have noticed that the Israelites followed Moses through the pathway in the Red Sea that God had prepared for his people. This may have been a frightening experience for many, but they trusted their God and their great leader Moses. However, when the godless Egyptians followed their foolish leaders along the same pathway they were destroyed. The Egyptian leaders were blind leaders of the blind, just as were the Pharisees in the time of Christ.

We must know what the Bible teaches, for there are many false teachers about today who are like the Pharisees — spiritually blind. If we follow such people, we shall be like a group of blind people trying to follow each other. When the leader falls into the ditch, the others follow.

Spiritually blind people are walking a pathway that leads to hell. Following such leaders will mean that our destiny is hell also. We must dare to be different from the godless people of this world. We must beware of following those who tell us that if we do the best we can, God will open the doors of heaven for us. People who teach this way to heaven are spiritually blind.

Let us all be true followers of the Lord Jesus Christ, ever trusting in his saving work alone in order that we may be loved of God and so be saved.

Activities

a. Whom do you know who tells you what to do?
b. Why should leaders be very careful in what they ask others to do?
c. Who is to blame when a leader tells you to do something wrong and you do it?

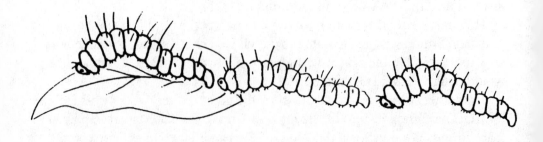

April Fool!

Read
Jeremiah 6:1-15

'They have also healed the hurt of My people slightly, saying, "Peace, peace!" when there is no peace' (Jeremiah 6:14).

It is sad, but true, that people tell lies and these lies can have a great effect upon us. In most English-speaking countries there is a special day of the year when practical jokes are played and everyone has to be on guard. That day is 'April Fools' Day', which falls on the first day of April each year.

At school everyone is wide awake as people are trying to trick each other. Sometimes a child would come and say something quite untrue: 'Quick, Sir, there's been an accident behind the bicycle shed!' Of course the teachers would have to check it out, just in case there had been an accident and someone needed help.

The principal of the school where I was teaching didn't think much of children playing practical jokes on teach-

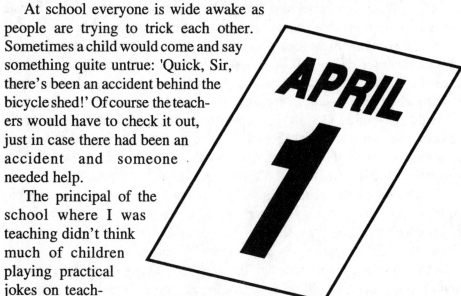

ers. He was ever on guard to make sure that no one caught him out. But the teachers usually enjoyed the time as much as the children.

One of the teachers said on the evening before April Fools' Day, 'How about playing a joke on John [the school principal] tomorrow morning?' All of the teachers thought that this would be a great idea, although no one was really keen on being the one to play the trick. However, one teacher volunteered.

At about 5:00 a.m., when it was still very dark, the teacher, who happened to be the deputy principal, rang the principal and said, 'John, I hope I didn't wake you up, but I've had a phone call from one of the school cleaners. She said that one of the water-pipes has broken and there is water flooding the playground. She rang me, but you're the school principal and I thought you should know.'

Poor old John thanked his deputy very much and declared that he would take care of it. He struggled out of bed and dressed himself for the ride down to the school. John always rode a small motorbike to school and at 5:00 a.m. it was very cold as he rode towards the school buildings.

When he arrived at school, he began to search for the cleaners. Of course when he found a cleaner she said that she knew nothing about a burst water-pipe. John looked about the playground, but could find no burst water-pipe.

Suddenly he realized what day it was. He was not very impressed as he rode his bike back to his home at that early hour. And his wife was not impressed with the teachers playing a practical joke on her husband. After all, he was the principal of the school.

In the staffroom that morning much laughter could be heard as the teachers spoke about the practical joke they had played on the school principal. When John arrived at school he had a smile on his face. He was not angry any more, and everyone seemed to have a good day.

That joke involved saying something that was untrue and we must beware of liars. Every reader of this book should be considered totally trustworthy in all they speak. The sad thing is that so often we cannot tell when a person is lying until it is too late. Some lies cause great heartache.

In the Scriptures, God warns us to beware of people who tell lies. In the days of the prophet Jeremiah there were false prophets. Jeremiah had warned the rebellious Jews of the coming judgement of God upon them. But the false prophets claimed that God would never hurt his special people.

God's prophets had called upon the people of Israel and Judah to repent of their sins, but the false prophets said there was nothing to worry about. Jeremiah tells us in our text that the false prophets were telling lies, saying, 'Peace, peace!' when there was no chance of peace.

So many of the people believed their lies. They thought all would be well. But of course there would be no peace, for the people would not repent and

144

the judgement of God would surely come. The people of Judah were taken into captivity in Babylon for seventy years. This was a terrible punishment for disobeying God and believing the lies of the false prophets.

There are people today, even ministers in the churches, who preach doctrines that are not true. Some tell us that because God is a God of love, he will never punish anyone. They say, 'Peace, peace!' when there is not going to be peace. They forget to warn people that our God is a just God who will punish all sinners who have not repented and live by faith in Christ.

Some would tell us that it doesn't matter what we believe, as long as we are sincere in what we believe. They assure us that all will be well when we stand before the judgement-seat of Christ. But this is not true. Jesus said, 'I am the way, the truth, and the life. No one comes to the Father except through Me' (John 14:6). There is a coming judgement and only those who trust in Christ will enter the kingdom of heaven.

Every one of you needs to know what the Bible teaches, for the Bible is the Word of God. Then when a false prophet tells his lies you will know the truth and not be led astray.

Activities

● ●

a. What jokes have people played on you?
b. Why must we be careful when we play a joke on another person?
c. Why should you always tell the truth?

Things are not always what they seem to be

...**Read** ....

Matthew 22:1-14

'Woe to you, scribes and Pharisees, hypocrites! For you are like whitewashed tombs which indeed appear beautiful outwardly, but inside are full of dead men's bones and all uncleanness. Even so you also outwardly appear righteous to men, but inside you are full of hypocrisy and lawlessness' (Matthew 23:27-28).

From some of my other stories you should realize that I love fishing. When my brother John lived about 150 kilometres away we would spend many days out at sea trying to catch the really big ones. And sometimes we caught very big fish. I remember once catching a ten-kilogram snapper. It was a lovely reddish-coloured fish, with a big, bony lump on its head. I took it home and very proudly showed the family. After it was scaled and gutted I carefully wrapped it in plastic and put the whole fish in the freezer. Now and again I would take it out and show any visitors the evidence of my fishing skill.

One day a friend who has a shop rang and asked if I had any large fish, as he wanted one for a special dinner he was preparing. It had to be a whole fish. I was so happy to say that I had just the fish he wanted. He was willing to pay good money for the fish, so I told him I would bring it to his shop.

When I began to lift the fish out of the freezer, I had a great shock! My lovely fish was not so lovely any more. It had its tail cut off. I called out to my wife, 'Whatever happened to my big snapper?'

She replied, 'I found it just too big to fit in the freezer, so now it fits in with ease.'

I was heartbroken. The fish was no good to the shop owner and certainly no good to show any visitors. We just had to eat it. The pride of my fishing trips was ruined.

There are many people in the world today who are proud. They like to pretend to be something they are not. Jesus had a lot of trouble with the Pharisees. They were the 'religious' people of that age. They pretended to be godly, and loved people to think that of them, but really they were not what they seemed to be. Jesus said they were 'hypocrites'. They were proud, but really they had nothing of which to be proud in the sight of God.

When I used to go out to sea fishing, I would tow the boat along a road where, nestled in the trees, I could see a lovely brick home. I often thought I would love to live close to the ocean in such a fine house. But one day my brother and I parked the car on the roadside near the home and had a close look.

To our surprise we discovered that the home was not what we thought it was. It was an old wooden house which just had a lovely brick front. A quick glance from the road, as we passed by, gave the wrong impression.

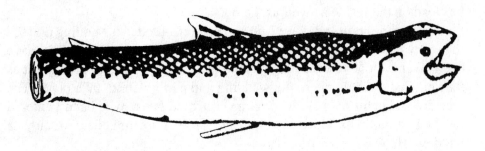

Jesus spoke angrily to the Pharisees who were not what they pretended to be. They made out that they loved God. They kept God's commandments as they thought they should be kept, as well as a lot of others they had invented. They believed that if they kept the commandments, God would owe them something. They were proud people and loved to have the ordinary people admiring them.

Jesus tells us that some of the proud Pharisees would, at the time of prayer, make sure that they were at a street corner (Matthew 6:5). Then they would stop, while others watched. They would hold their hands heavenwards and pray. The Jews standing about watching thought they were very godly people. But really, they were proud sinners, who had no love for the Son of God. They wanted Jesus dead. In our text Jesus compared them to graves which looked beautiful on the outside and yet under the beauty were decaying bodies and bones.

My wife Valerie and I had a holiday in Malaysia some time ago. A friend in my congregation was in the Australian Airforce, and for several years was stationed there. Peter and his wife Judy invited us over for a holiday.

On one of our trips into the countryside we came upon a small Chinese cemetery. The graves were very colourful. They had lovely patterned tiles on them and I'm sure the people who had built them must have been very proud of their work. They were so clean it was obvious that relatives had come to the cemetery to keep the area clean and the tiles polished. This small cemetery reminded me of the words of our text, spoken by Jesus. The graves looked beautiful on the outside, but were not very nice on the inside.

There are people today who make themselves out to be what they are not. They attend worship and pretend to be Christians, but in fact are just proud people who love themselves and not God.

We need to be cleansed on the inside as well as the outside. And the only way we can be truly cleansed on the inside is by the Holy Spirit coming and making his home in our hearts and souls. When we repent of our sins, the blood of Jesus Christ will wash them all away and in God's sight we shall be clean on the inside as well as the outside.

In our reading for today we find a man who attended a wedding dressed in his own clothes. In that bygone age all the wedding guests would have been given a cloak to wear. This would have been handed to each guest as they entered the hall where the wedding and party were to take place. The man dressed in his own clothes was an uninvited guest, who hadn't entered the hall through the doorway, but had probably climbed in through a window. He was a man who was very much out of place.

Reader, have a good look at yourself. If you say you are a believer in Christ, is this shown in your love for him? Do you honour God day by day? Do you obey the commandments — not to show others how good you think you are, but because you love Jesus Christ? Are you trusting in Christ's righteousness to get you to heaven? We need to be clothed, not in our own filthy clothes of our supposedly good works, but in clothing made from the perfect holiness of Christ.

We might be able to fool the people we know about our pretended love for Christ, but we cannot fool God. Jesus said, 'For there is nothing covered that will not be revealed, nor hidden that will not be known' (Luke 12:2).

Reader, may you be a true Christian, and not just a proud hypocrite.

Activities

● ●

a. Talk about something that is lovely on the outside and dirty on the inside.
b. Do you think people can look nice on the outside but inside be very unkind?
c. What sort of person are you? Do other people know you as you really are?

Angels

Read
2 Kings 6:8-23

'The angel of the Lord encamps all around those who fear Him, and delivers them' (Psalm 34:7).

Some people have the idea that when they die they will become angels in heaven. Those of you who know your Bible will understand that this is not so. Angels were created by God before our world was created. Before Adam and Eve walked in the Garden of Eden the angels in heaven worshipped God and carried out his commands.

Angels are spoken about hundreds of times throughout the Word of God; and it is good for you to understand who the angels are and what they do.

Our text tells us that the 'angel of the Lord' is the protector of the people of God. In fact we read in Hebrews 1:14 that the angels have a very special occupation. They are 'ministering spirits sent forth to minister for those who will inherit salvation'. In some way, the very angels of God do God's bidding, so that Christians might be blessed and protected from evil. It is wonderful to think that the angels of God are with us wherever we go, protecting us from Satan and his demons.

In 2 Kings 6 from verse 8, we find an interesting story about the angels who protected Elisha, the Lord's prophet. The King of Syria wanted to capture Elisha, so he sent a large army to the city of Dothan where Elisha and his servant were staying. Early one morning Elisha's servant went out to the city walls and to his horror saw the army of the King of Syria — soldiers, chariots and horses — camped around the city.

Elisha's servant cried out in fear, 'Alas, my master! What shall we do?' (v.15).

Elisha knew that the angels of God were there to protect him from the Syrian army. He prayed that God might open, in a very special way, the eyes of his servant. We read, 'Then the Lord opened the eyes of the young man, and he saw. And behold, the mountain was full of horses and chariots of fire all around Elisha' (v.17).

You read the whole story, and find out what happened to that great Syrian army. God, using his angels, protected Elisha and his servant.

Jesus told some parables about God searching out his people and saving them. He told the parables of 'the Lost Sheep', 'the Lost Coin' and 'the Prodigal Son' (Luke 15). Then Christ tells us that there is great joy in heaven when a sinner repents of his sins. In verse 10 we read, 'Likewise, I say to you, there is joy in the presence of the angels of God over one sinner who repents.' The angels are very concerned that the purposes of God are fulfilled. When they are, the angels rejoice. Do you realize that, if you are a Christian, the angels in heaven rejoiced over you, the day you believed?

Christ spoke about Lazarus and the rich man, and there (Luke 16:19-31) we are told that the very angels of heaven were with godly Lazarus when he died. We read, 'So it was that the beggar died, and was carried by the angels to Abraham's bosom' (v. 22). Isn't this wonderful? When God's people are dying, the angels are there ready to carry the soul into the presence of Christ.

Sometimes when we read of the work of the angels, we tend to think to ourselves, 'That all happened in another place and another time. Those sort of things don't happen now.'

I would like to tell you a story that I read in a book titled *Angels: God's Secret Agents* by Billy Graham (Doubleday & Co., New York, 1975, p.3.). The story is about the Reverend John G. Paton, who was a missionary in the New Hebrides Islands. Billy Graham writes:

The Reverend John G. Paton, a missionary in the New Hebrides Islands, tells a thrilling story involving the protective care of angels. Hostile natives surrounded his mission headquarters one night, intent on burning the Patons out and killing them. John Paton and his wife prayed all during that terror-filled night that God would deliver them. When daylight came they were amazed to see the attackers unaccountably leave. They thanked God for delivering them.

A year later, the chief of the tribe was converted to Jesus Christ, and Mr Paton, remembering what had happened, asked the chief what had kept him and his men from burning down the house and killing them. The chief replied in surprise, 'Who were all those men you had with you there?' The missionary answered, 'There were no men there; just my wife and I.' The chief argued that they had seen many men standing guard — hundreds of big men in shining garments with drawn swords in their hands. They seemed to circle the mission station so that the natives were afraid to attack. Only then did Mr Paton realize that God had sent his angels to protect them. The chief agreed that there was no other explanation.

Billy Graham then asks the question: 'Could it be that God had sent a legion of angels to protect his servants, whose lives were being endangered?'

When the Lord Jesus Christ was in the Garden of Gethsemane, just before his trial and crucifixion, we read that he knelt down, and in great agony, prayed to his heavenly Father. He knew that his death by crucifixion was soon to be. He also knew that his death would be most horrible, for he would be carrying the sins of his people, and so be punished by God in their place. He prayed, 'Father, if it is Your will, remove this cup from Me; nevertheless not My will, but Yours, be done' (Luke 22:42). In the verse that follows we then read, 'Then an angel appeared to Him from heaven, strengthening Him.'

What a wonderful event! God had sent one of his angels to his Son Jesus to give him courage and strength to die for his people.

Reader, if you are a Christian, you will one day have the opportunity of meeting that very angel who appeared to Christ in the Garden of Gethsemane.

God's angels are about us to protect us. Praise God!

Activities

● ●

a. What is an angel?
b. Tell a story about angels that is found in the Bible.
c. Did Mum, Dad or someone in your family ever say you are an angel?
   Why?
d. Are you really an angel?

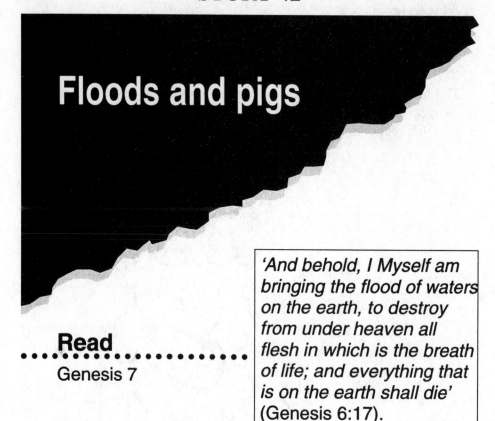

Floods and pigs

Read
....
Genesis 7

'And behold, I Myself am bringing the flood of waters on the earth, to destroy from under heaven all flesh in which is the breath of life; and everything that is on the earth shall die' (Genesis 6:17).

The story of Noah and the great flood is frightening, because it reminds us that God hates sin and will punish sinners. Every time we look up into the heavens and see the rainbow, we should be reminded of that great flood, and of God's promise that he would never again destroy the world by water. The next time the world is destroyed it will be by fire and that will happen at the time of Christ's return.

In those early days following creation and Adam and Eve's fall into sin, men and women became more wicked. They hated God and were very cruel to one another. They wanted to live without any thought of God. They just wanted to please themselves and live for pleasure. The Bible tells us that when God saw the terrible wickedness of mankind he was even sorry that he had created man (Genesis 6:5-6).

God was determined to destroy the world by flood. But there was one righteous man and his family whom God would save — that was Noah and his wife, their sons and their wives.

How the wicked people must have laughed at Noah and his family as they began to build that huge boat, the ark, just as God had commanded them to do! The people of that age couldn't imagine what a flood would be like as

154

the Bible tells us that there had not been rain on the land till the time of Noah. We are told that the earth was watered by a mist (Genesis 2:5-6).

I'm sure you all have read about, or seen on television, great floods that have ruined many parts of the earth. When I was young, we lived on a farm and every couple of years there would be a flood. The floods did a lot of damage, but they did some good, because the flood water washed good soil down from the mountains and deposited it on the flood plains. The flood soil was very good for growing crops.

As children my brother and I usually enjoyed the flood, even though Mum and Dad were heartbroken when they saw the farm crops destroyed. My brother and I used to swim in the water and we had a boat in which we rowed about. All in all, John and I had a great time in the floods. It even meant that we missed out on school for a couple of weeks.

One year there was a very big flood and for the first time the flood water entered our home to a depth of about two metres. This ruined our furniture, our clothes and we lost many things that we held precious. Probably the things we lost and miss most of all were the photographs of us when we were young.

Our home was built several metres above ground level and we had a huge hay shed that had also been built up several metres. When we knew that this flood was going to be very bad, we moved all of our cattle to higher ground. Then we had to stack the house furniture up as high as we could hoping to save it, but we couldn't get things high enough.

We were able to move all of our animals except a pig. Now this pig had a sty beside the hay shed. He was quite big and didn't like humans at all. He wouldn't let anyone pat him on the back and if we got too close he would put his head down and rush at us. Dad said that one day he would make good bacon.

When we tried to move all of the animals the wicked pig would not go. He kept running away and every now and again would put his head down and rush at whoever was nearest to him. Eventually Dad said, 'Well, old fellow, you can just take your chances in the flood.' So the pig stayed behind when all of the cattle were moved. The water was rising and before nightfall, Dad said we had better leave the pigsty gate open.

In the morning water was everywhere, metres deep. The water was not in the house at that stage, but as we were eating breakfast someone asked, 'I wonder what has happened to the pig?' We all moved to the window and looked out. The pigsty was well and truly under water and Dad said, 'I guess he's been drowned. We won't get our bacon.' But as we looked across the water into the hay shed, we could see the pig, alive and well.

In the hay shed there was an old flat-bottomed boat that was good for nothing. To our amazement there was the pig standing on the bottom of the

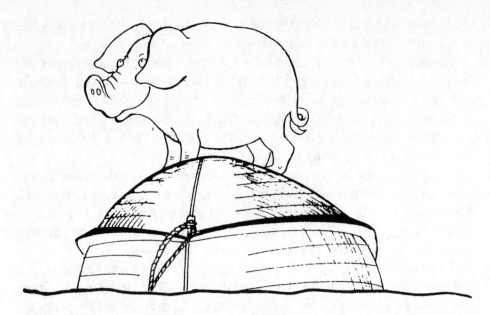

upturned boat, balancing himself very carefully. We could see some small waves running into the shed and rocking the boat, but the pig seemed to know just what to do to prevent the boat rolling over. How he got himself to the boat and then onto the bottom we could only guess, but there he was.

Daily we had to row our large flood boat up to the hill country to milk the cows and Dad suggested that before we left we might once again try and rescue that 'hard to get on with' pig.

We rowed our boat towards the pig as he balanced on the upturned boat. If he'd been on the ground he would have run away or put his head down and charged us. That pig really hated humans, but this time it seemed as if his whole nature was changed. The closer we got to him, we could almost see a smile of relief on his face. He didn't try to back away from us, but when we were close, he very carefully began to walk along the bottom of his boat towards our outstretched hands.

He came so close that eventually we could touch his head and then we half lifted him as he jumped into our boat. He looked at us as if to say, 'Thank you.' Then he flopped down on the bottom of our boat for he was really exhausted. He'd probably been awake all night, balancing himself on the upturned boat. We rescued that wicked, hard to get on with pig.

When God destroyed the world by that great flood of Noah's day, the wicked people were destroyed. Godly Noah and his family were saved. And we are told that when they and the animals were safe and secure in the ark, God closed the door. No one else could gain safety there. The world of wickedness outside perished.

We know that God will again destroy this world, and next time by fire. But who will be saved when that happens? The answer is given in Scripture.

We read the apostle Paul's words to the Philippian jailer — words that apply to us: 'Believe on the Lord Jesus Christ, and you will be saved...' (Acts 16:31).

All who trust in the Lord Jesus Christ will be saved on that day. Jesus Christ will be to his people what that ark was to Noah. Jesus is the rock of our salvation. Trust in him, reader, and you will be spiritually safe, not only in this world, but throughout all of eternity.

Activities

a. How many people were on Noah's ark?
b. Who closed the door of the ark?
c. What do you think the people said to Noah when he and his family were building the ark?
d. Why would they say such things?
e. What does the story of Noah and the flood teach you?

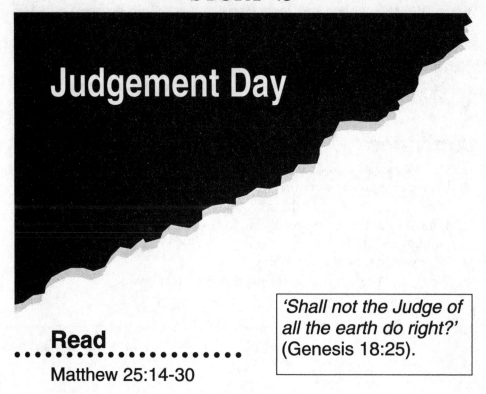

Judgement Day

Read
....
Matthew 25:14-30

'Shall not the Judge of all the earth do right?' (Genesis 18:25).

Our text is found in that part of the Bible where the Lord told Abraham that he was going to destroy the cities of Sodom and Gomorrah because of their terrible wickedness. Abraham was afraid that God would destroy, with fire and brimstone, both the wicked and the righteous people of the city. He pleaded with God that he might save all the godly people of Sodom. In fact he politely argued with God, 'Would You destroy the righteous with the wicked? Suppose there were fifty righteous within the city; would You destroy the place and not spare it for the fifty righteous that were in it...?' (Genesis 18:23-24).

Abraham continued to plead with God, eventually saying, '"Let not the Lord be angry, and I will speak but once more: Suppose ten should be found there?" And He said, "I will not destroy it for the sake of ten"' (Genesis 18:32).

One of the arguments Abraham used when he was reasoning with God is found in the words of our text: 'Shall not the Judge of all the earth do right?' Now I feel sure that at some time in your life, you have been treated in an unfair manner. I would like to tell you about an incident in my family, where I treated one of my daughters unfairly. There is a lesson here for us all.

Our girls loved to play games in their bedrooms. They would often get the bed clothes and make a cubby house by hanging the blankets over the bunk-bed and then pretending that it was their home. They would put their toys in the cubby house, make pretend cups of tea and ask their Mum and Dad to come and join them in their games.

Sometimes they would put sheets over their heads and pretend they were ghosts and try to scare everyone. And even though they made a lot of noise, they were having harmless fun.

One day, however, the noise was not as loud as it had been. Everything suddenly became quiet. Then we heard some little giggles coming from one of the bedrooms. My wife said to me, 'Those girls are up to something. Please put your head around the door and see what is going on.' Isn't it strange how mothers and fathers expect the worst when the children become quiet?

Well, I popped my head around the door to find the girls with sheets over their heads; but not all — one had a lovely blanket over her head. Then I noticed a pair of scissors on the floor and asked: 'What's going on? What have you been doing with the scissors?'

Before they could answer I suddenly saw two eyes looking at me through some holes cut in the blanket. One of the girls had cut out holes for two eyes, a nose and a mouth. I was horrified. A good blanket was spoiled. Now we knew why everything was quiet. Someone knew they had done something wrong.

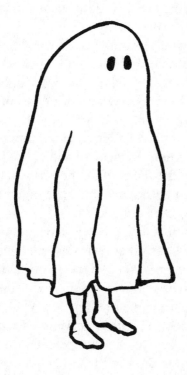

I pulled the blanket off the one hiding under it. There was poor little Cathie. 'I didn't do it!' she exclaimed.

My wife and I carried out an investigation. All of the girls said they were innocent, but to me it looked like Cathie was the guilty one and so she was the one who got into trouble. For a long time she told me that she wasn't the one who had cut the holes in the blanket.

One day, many years later, when we were all laughing about things that happened when the children were young, Cathie said, 'Dad, do you remember the day you blamed me for cutting the holes in the blanket?'

I replied, 'Yes, I can remember that day. Were you really the guilty one?' Then Heather spoke up. She said, 'Dad, I was the one who did it, but we agreed that we wouldn't tell.'

Well, I had to say to Cathie, 'I'm sorry Cathie. I sure made a mistake that time.'

Thinking back to that day, it brought to my mind the great truth that one day every person alive will be judged by God, through his dear Son Jesus Christ. The Bible tells us that the Lord Jesus will return and that all must appear before his judgement-seat. I made a mistake in my judgement of Cathie, and so my punishment was all wrong. The guilty one escaped punishment.

We read in the Bible that God 'will judge the world in righteousness by the Man he has ordained. He has given assurance of this to all by raising Him from the dead' (Acts 17:31). God will make no mistakes in his judgement, because he knows all of the facts. Nothing can be hidden from him on that day.

The prophet Jeremiah tells us things that should put fear into our hearts. We read, 'The heart is deceitful above all things, and desperately wicked; who can know it? I the Lord, search the heart, I test the mind, even to give every man according to his ways, and according to the fruit of his doings' (Jeremiah 17:9-10). God not only sees what we do, but he knows the very reasons why we act the way we do. He can look into our hearts and minds.

Because of this, God's judgement of all humans will be perfectly fair. As Abraham said, 'Shall not the Judge of all the earth do right?' How will you feel when your name is called out and you have to move forward, before all of mankind, and face the Lord Jesus Christ?

Reader, I pray that on that day, you will have a true joy in your heart. If you are trusting in the Saviour, all of your sins will have been removed from you. The one who is the Judge is your Saviour, who has borne the punishment for your sins. You will be clothed, not in your sins, but in his perfect righteousness. If you are truly one of Christ's people, your judgement will be one of: 'Well done, good and faithful servant... Enter into the joy of your Lord' (Matthew 25:21). But to the unrepentant sinners, who trusted in anything and everything but the Lord Jesus, he will say the terrible words:

'Depart from Me, you cursed, into the everlasting fire prepared for the devil and his angels' (Matthew 25:41).

How will things be with you, reader, on that great day when Christ comes again? I pray that you all are living the life of faith in preparation for your meeting with the 'King of Kings and Lord of Lords' (Revelation 19:16).

Activities

●●

a. Are you always fair when you say something about other people?
b. How do you know you haven't made a mistake in your judgements of other people?
c. Will you be saved on judgement day? Give the reasons for your answer?

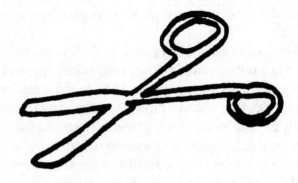

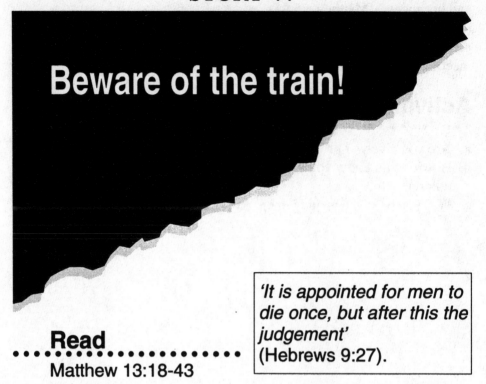

Beware of the train!

Read
• • • • • • • • • • • • • • • • • • •
Matthew 13:18-43

'It is appointed for men to die once, but after this the judgement' (Hebrews 9:27).

The words above should make everyone stop and think. It is a fact that unless the Lord Jesus returns first, we shall all one day die. Our life on this earth will come to an end and all of the things that we treasured here will be left behind for someone else to use. Many people believe that the grave is the end and that when a body is buried that is the end of that person. They believe the person does not exist any more.

Because of this, people in this world live to satisfy themselves. The Bible says their aim in life is to 'eat, drink and be merry' (Luke 12:19). They live as if they alone mattered and so make no preparation for meeting God after they die.

They are like some boys I heard of who used to play around some railway yards at a railway siding. They loved climbing over the railway trucks and sometimes even an engine would be found there for them to clamber over.

One day they found a railway trolley that railway workers used to travel along the line to their places of work. The trolley had a short handle that could be moved backwards and forwards to turn the wheels. A couple of the boys found it quite easy to get the trolley moving. However, they normally only used the trolley in the safety of the railway siding.

One day they decided to do something really foolish. They believed the train only travelled the lines once a day, about mid-afternoon. So they decided to take the trolley for a real run along the tracks. They would do this in the morning because they thought there would be no train at that time of the day. Somehow they were able to move the railway points and get the trolley onto the main railway line.

Well, they had great fun racing the trolley backwards and forwards on the lines. In fact they even went for more than a kilometre along the tracks. To them it sure was great fun. They had not a care in the world. No trains, just great excitement filled their morning.

But all was not well, for they did not know that a special train was running that morning. They were several kilometres from the safety of the railway siding when, around a bend in the railway lines, a train came thundering towards them. It was travelling very fast, and so were they. And they were both heading for each other.

They thought they were safe, but now they were in serious danger. With all their might they slowed the trolley down, while the train driver blew the whistle. The wheels of the train were screeching and the perspiration was pouring from the faces of the frightened boys. Just before the train hit the trolley the boys jumped for their lives. They were safe, but the train smashed the trolley to pieces.

The boys didn't wait to find out what happened next. They just ran as fast as they could for the trees and then quietly made their way home. They were most fortunate to still be alive. Those boys never went down to the railway tracks again. They were too frightened.

Today, many people live like those boys. They cannot see the coming judgement of God. They think that all is well. They believe that the grave is the end, but how foolish!

Our text tells us the plain truth: 'It is appointed for men to die once, but after this the judgement.' The Judgement Day of God is coming whether we like it or not. One day we shall each stand before the judgement-seat of Christ to give an account of our lives to the just Judge of heaven and earth. Thinking that the grave is the end of human existence will not save us from the Judgement Day. And if we have not made preparation for that day we shall be the most foolish of people.

The only preparation you can make for the Day of Judgement is to trust in the saving work of the Lord Jesus Christ. If this is what you have done, then praise God, for he made it possible for you to believe. You have faith because God loved you and sent his Holy Spirit into your heart. It is the saving work of the Holy Spirit that makes it possible for a person to believe in Christ and repent of his or her sins.

Those foolish boys received a terrible shock when the train that wasn't supposed to be there suddenly appeared. They were fortunate to keep their lives as they saw their danger just in time. But if, before you die, you make no true preparation for the Judgement Day, your death will mean that all hope is gone. There are no second chances after death to trust in the Lord.

Our reading today tells us very clearly that when Christ returns in power he will send forth his angels to gather together all who are unrepentant sinners: 'those who offend, and those who practise lawlessness' (Matthew 13:41). These, we are told, will be cast into hell. What a terrible thing it will be on Judgement Day for you, if you have rejected God's salvation through faith in Christ!

Paul wrote, 'Behold, now is the accepted time; behold, now is the day of salvation' (2 Corinthians 6:2). Today could be our last day on earth. Today we could die and then face the judgement-seat of Christ. If you are not prepared for that then get down on your knees, and ask Jesus to send his Spirit into your heart and give you saving faith.

Activities

a. Do you know that some day everybody must die?
b. What does the Bible tell us always follows death?
c. How can you prepare for the day of your death?

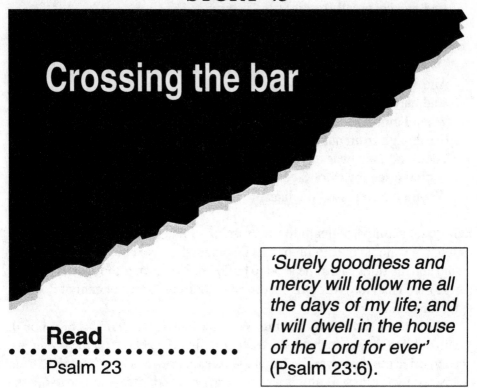

Crossing the bar

Read
••••••••••••••••••••
Psalm 23

'Surely goodness and mercy will follow me all the days of my life; and I will dwell in the house of the Lord for ever' (Psalm 23:6).

Psalm 23 is the best-known psalm in the Bible. It was written by David, who became the second king of Israel. In his young days David was a shepherd who looked after his father's sheep. He would protect them from the wild animals who would kill and eat the defenceless animals. David would make sure that the sheep were taken to places where there was water to drink and plenty of green grass to eat.

In this psalm David compares the Lord to a shepherd. Just as the shepherd cares for the sheep, so David tells us that God will care for his people. During our earthly lives God has promised to faithfully protect us as far as our faith in Christ is concerned. We might suffer at the hands of the wicked, godless people of this world, but God will keep us spiritually safe.

One of the most wonderful things that will happen to all of God's people, the saints, is that when they die, or Christ returns, they will live with the Lord Jesus in the home he has prepared for them. Today God's people enter heaven through death and I want to say something about dying.

Alfred Lord Tennyson was a great English poet who wrote a poem called 'Crossing the bar'. Below are some lines of his poem.

Sunset and evening star,
And one clear call for me!
And may there be no moaning of the bar,
When I put out to sea...
Twilight and evening bell,
And after that the dark!
And may there be no sadness of farewell,
When I embark;
For though from out our borne of Time and Place
The flood may bear me far,
I hope to see my Pilot face to face
When I have crossed the bar.

This poem compares death to the crossing of a bar. Now a bar is a shallow stretch of water at the mouth of a river, where the river enters the ocean. The wind and the tides cause the sand to build up. Sometimes the sand will build up so much that the river will become blocked and the water cannot flow out into the ocean.

My brother and I enjoy fishing. We once had a boat that was big enough to go out into the sea to catch the really big fish. To get out on the ocean, we had to drive the boat over the bar at the river entrance. Many boats had been capsized by rough seas and it was necessary to take great care crossing the bar. At low tide the waves were usually very big.

We had crossed the bar many times. Sometimes the ocean there was so smooth that we had no problem at all. We just went down the river in our boat, across the smooth bar, and out onto the ocean where there were no waves at all. Sometimes when we reached the bar the waves were so big, we were too frightened to cross it. We just turned the boat around and went home.

One morning, before the sun was up, we arrived at the bar. The water looked safe enough but as we waited for a few minutes we noticed that every now and again a big wave would build up. However, we thought we could take great care and get out safely. The water in the river was very calm, and the water out to sea was smooth.

My brother stood at the bow of the boat to keep watch on the waves at the bar, while I stood up behind the boat's steering wheel. John was to tell me when it was safe to go. I would then open the throttle of the outboard and off we'd go, across the bar, while there were no waves.

Suddenly John shouted, 'Go!'

I opened the throttle of the outboard and the boat sped towards the bar. The water looked calm and I was sure all would be well. But just as we reached the shallow water, a huge wave appeared in front of us. Our boat was really speeding, so there was nothing I could do but keep going. I held onto the steering wheel with all my might, while John flopped into his seat and hung on tightly.

Our boat went up that wave and flew out of the top. We just floated in space for a few seconds before hitting the water with a terrible thump. The motor was roaring so very fast that the boat shot ahead like a rocket when it landed.

I fell over my seat and landed at the back of the boat. I looked at my hands and found I still had more than half of the steering wheel firmly grasped between my fingers. I jumped to my feet, grabbed the remaining spoke of the steering wheel and guided the boat out to sea, into the very calm water.

I didn't think much of John, the pilot, who had shouted out, 'Go!' but we were now safe on the wide, blue ocean. We had a great day at sea, where we caught many good fish.

Tennyson compares death to the crossing of a bar. Sometimes death can be so easy that there are no difficulties. Sometimes death can be troublesome, like the rough bar; but we must all cross that bar which is called death, unless the Lord Jesus returns first. Remember that the Scriptures tell us that only two humans entered heaven without passing through death. Open your Bible and read about Enoch (Genesis 5:24), and Elijah (2 Kings 2:1-11). God will be with us in our death, so all Christians need not fear dying. In Psalm 116:15 we read some wonderful words: 'Precious in the sight of the Lord is the death of his saints.'

Jesus has promised all of his people that he will never leave them nor forsake them — not even at the time of their death. But when we cross the 'bar' — death — there are many wonderful things waiting for us, and the poet Tennyson wrote of the best of all. He said:

I hope to see my Pilot face to face
When I have crossed the bar.

Reader, do you notice something about the word 'Pilot'? It is written with a capital letter, because Tennyson is speaking about Jesus.

When the big ships were to cross a bar they had a pilot to guide them safely into and out of the harbour. So also with Jesus our Saviour. He will guide us home to be with himself for ever.

Christ has told his disciples something very precious, and his words apply to all of his people as well. He said in John 14:1-3: 'Let not your heart be troubled; you believe in God, believe also in Me. In My Father's house are many mansions; if it were not so, I would have told you. I go to prepare a place for you. And if I go and prepare a place for you, I will come again and receive you to Myself; that where I am, there you may be also.'

Reader, you may be happy so far in your life, but one day you will die. If you belong to Jesus you can say, 'The best is yet to be!'

Activities
• •

a. Why is it that Christians need not fear death?
b. What happens when a Christian dies?
c. How would you feel if some Christian you loved died?

Concorde arrives

Jesus said, *'Behold, I am coming as a thief. Blessed is he who watches...'* (Revelation 16:15).

....Read...............
Matthew 24:32-44

Two of my friends, Jim and Rex, had a great interest in aeroplanes. They took every opportunity to talk about planes, to read about planes and to visit airports. They had been airmen in the wartime and had flown in bombers.

I don't really like aeroplanes because I'm not very happy when my feet move off the ground. Several times I've had to travel by plane, but have always sat on a seat in the middle of the plane, where I couldn't see out of the window. And when the plane was taking off or landing, the palms of my hands became very sweaty. But my two aeroplane-loving friends were not at all like me. They just loved aeroplanes!

One day we read in the newspaper that a new aeroplane was to visit Australia — it was the newly built *Concorde*. This plane was going to fly non-stop from England to Australia. My two friends talked about *Concorde* for a long time, telling each other what a great plane it must be.

I wasn't surprised when they told me they had decided to travel by train to Sydney, where *Concorde* would land. They were so excited about the trip they were to make, and thrilled that they would see for themselves the great bird-like *Concorde*.

When they returned home I asked them what the trip was like. All they could speak of was the arrival of the great aeroplane. Jim said, 'There were thousands of people at Mascot airport. It was a cloudy day and everyone was looking upwards just waiting for the plane to break through the clouds. We all strained our eyes in silence, just waiting. Then suddenly the plane appeared. Everyone began to clap and talk. It was wonderful to see the plane land and to be able to get close to it.'

A day or so later there were pictures in the newspapers, showing the thousands of people standing together, looking upwards and waiting.

This picture reminded me that one day the Lord Jesus Christ will return to this world. He will not come in secret, for the Bible tells us, 'And every eye will see Him…' (Revelation 1:7). When I saw the picture of thousands waiting for the arrival of *Concorde* I wondered just how many people are really waiting for the Lord Jesus Christ to come. I wonder if you are looking upwards and praying that today might be the day when our Saviour returns.

Our text tells us that Christ will return when most people are not expecting him to come. Indeed, the Lord Jesus tells us that on the day that he returns, people will be going about their normal tasks. He said, 'Then two men will be in the field: one will be taken and the other left. Two women will be grinding at the mill: one will be taken and the other left. Watch therefore, for you do not know what hour your Lord is coming' (Matthew 24:40-42).

The message of the Bible is that Jesus Christ, the Son of God, who was abused by wicked men and nailed to a cross 2,000 years ago, is coming again as a great King, to judge the world in righteousness.

The warning of the Bible is that all should be ready for his return. And the way we can prepare for the coming of Christ, is to trust in him as our only Saviour and to daily live a godly life.

What a wonderful day it will be for all of God's people, when Christ returns! Suddenly the heavens will be torn apart, there will be the shout of the archangel and everyone will look towards the heavens. And there will be our Saviour Jesus Christ coming as the great King to take his people home.

The apostle Peter wrote of the return of Christ and said that when he returns the world will be burned up. Then there will be a wonderful new creation for God's people to live in. Peter warns us as to how we are to prepare for the coming of Christ: 'But the day of the Lord will come as a thief in the night, in which the heavens will pass away with a great noise, and the elements will melt with fervent heat; both the earth and the works that are in it will be burned up. Therefore, since all these things will be dissolved, what manner of persons ought you to be in holy conduct and godliness…?' (2 Peter 3:10-11).

Activities

a. Do you know the date of Jesus' return to earth? Why?
b. How should you live in preparation for the return of Christ?
c. What will happen when Jesus returns?

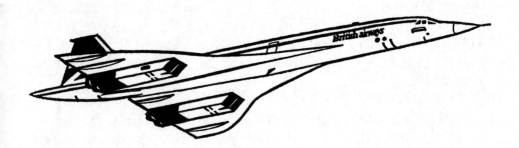

'I've been here for ever!'

> **Read**
> • • • • • • • • • • • • • • • • • • •
> Revelation 20:7-15

> 'And these will go away into everlasting punishment, but the righteous into eternal life' (Matthew 25:46).

Many times in the Bible we read the word 'everlasting', and I'm sure we don't think much about the meaning of this word. As we look at ourselves and our surroundings, we find that things change and that nothing seems to last very long. To read that someone or something is everlasting confuses our minds, because we can't understand it.

The Bible tells us that God is everlasting. We read in Psalm 93:2: 'Your throne is established from of old; You are from everlasting.'

Our God is eternal, but not only that, we read that our God does not change. In Psalm 102:25-27 we read, 'Of old You laid the foundation of the earth, and the heavens are the work of Your hands. They will perish, but You will endure; yes, all of them will grow old like a garment; like a cloak You will change them. And they will be changed. But You are the same, and Your years will have no end.'

There is no doubt that we grow old and change. Every time I look in the mirror I can see what hair I have left turning grey. I once had a good head of black hair, but this has changed now. I've had to buy some new trousers which are somewhat bigger than the previous ones. I am changing daily, but God never changes. My life and your life had a beginning, but God is eternal — he had no beginning nor has he an end to his existence.

But we must always remember that our existence does not end when we die and our body is laid in the grave. We shall live for ever in one of two places — in the new creation with Christ, or in hell with the devil and his angels. 'For ever' is a long time!

One day, when I was teaching at a large city school, one of the teachers entered the staffroom at lunch-time, laughing. Someone asked, 'What's funny?'

'You wouldn't believe it,' he replied, 'but this morning after we went into school Peter Smith wouldn't keep quiet. I just took hold of him, stood him out of the way behind the door and told him not to make a sound or he'd be in really serious trouble.'

'Well,' someone asked, 'what's funny with that?'

The teacher replied, 'I forgot I put him there and just before lunch, when the class was ready to go out, Peter very quietly poked his head out from behind the door and said, "Sir, may I have lunch too? I've been here for ever!" He'd been standing there for about three hours.'

Poor young Peter. It must have seemed a long time behind the door, but it certainly wasn't for ever. It is hard to imagine what is meant by 'for ever'. I'll try to explain what for ever is like.

I love fishing and used to have my own boat to go to sea in. The ocean is a very large place and there's a lot of water for boats to float about on.

Just imagine this. I give you a small bucket and tell you that you have a special job to do. You must fill your bucket with salty ocean water and pour it into a dam nearby. It only takes about ten minutes to get a bucketful and tip it into the reservoir. This means you empty 144 buckets full of water each day, 1,008 each week, and 52,416 each year. Now when you have totally emptied the oceans and seas of their water, you have just started the first moment of eternity.

Eternity is a very long time!

In our text Jesus is describing the end of all humanity. We shall spend eternity in either heaven or hell. Heaven is the dwelling-place of God, the home of the saints and the place of righteousness.

Hell is the eternal dwelling-place of all who have not repented of their sins and trusted in Jesus Christ for salvation. And there are no second chances for those in hell. Hell is the place of 'everlasting punishment'. That is why hell is called 'the second death' (Revelation 20:14).

There is no fun and laughter in hell. And I'm sure that there will be two words often spoken by hell's inhabitants: 'If only...'

When Jesus spoke of eternal life he was not only speaking of the length of our life, but he was also speaking of the quality of that life. Living in the home that God has prepared for his people will be a true life of joy and happiness. There will be no death or pain there, because there is no evil in the new heavens and the new earth. And all of God's people will spend eternity exploring and enjoying what God has prepared for his people. We shall sing his praises and worship him for ever.

Let us ever remember that none of God's people has earned the right to enter heaven. We shall only enter heaven because of Christ's life of perfect obedience, and his death in our place, bearing our sins.

In heaven we shall praise our Saviour for ever and ever.

And for ever is a long time!

Activities

• •

a. Over the past few years what changes have you noticed in one person you love?

b. I can't understand what eternity means. Make up a story like mine that tells you that eternity is time unending.

c. Why are the words 'If only...' so very sad?

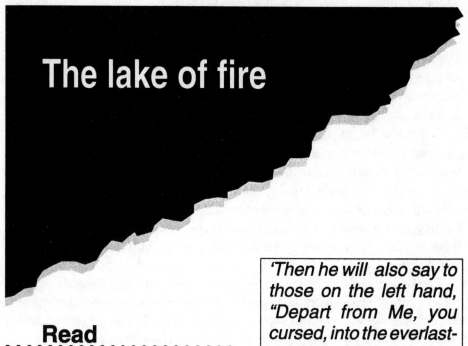

The lake of fire

Read
Revelation 14:6-13
and Luke 16:19-31

'Then he will also say to those on the left hand, "Depart from Me, you cursed, into the everlasting fire prepared for the devil and his angels"' (Matthew 25:41).

A fire can sometimes be a good friend and at other times a real enemy. When I was young, a friend and I belonged to the Sea Scouts. Our scout troop had a large boat which we used for rowing about in the river. It was always great fun to get together every second Friday evening for scout meetings and the many games we used to play. We learned how to tie knots; we were taught water safety and many other things that were of use to us as scouts.

One night the scout leader announced that we would all be going on a camping trip. We would row the scout boat several miles up the river and camp overnight in a deserted school shelter shed. The school had been closed for many years and the school building had been removed. But beside a huge fig tree was a small shelter shed. That would be our camping site.

When the day arrived, about ten boys set out with the scout leader. We happily rowed the boat up the river, thinking about the great time we were going to have. We arrived at the camp-site just before dark — in time to gather some sticks for a fire. Over the fire we cooked sausages and boiled water for some tea to drink. Everything was great.

When night fell, we sat around the fire singing songs. Eventually, it was time for sleep. The fire was dying down, but no one really felt tired. We were all too excited.

But as the night wore on the coldness set in. Even now, I can still remember how cold I felt those forty-five years ago. The fire was nearly out. The moon was glowing in the dark sky, and the frost was beginning to settle on the ground. I can remember my teeth starting to chatter with the cold. It was so cold that no one could settle down to sleep. Our blankets did not keep us warm, so we all began to move closer to the fire that was nearly out.

Some of us began to stumble about in the dark looking for more firewood, and every now and again someone would bring back a stick and the fire would burn brightly for a time. The side of our bodies that faced the fire would get too hot but the other side was just so cold.

I still remember sitting there watching the fire and the moon. I was longing for the sun to rise and give us some warmth. And we all shivered there together, till eventually the sun rose over the hills and we began to get warm again.

The fire helped us a little that night. But fires can cause great damage. In New South Wales, Australia, in early 1994 tremendous bushfires raged for more than a week. 185 homes were totally destroyed and many hundreds of homes were badly damaged. Some people died in the flames and lots of bush animals met their death. Thousands of acres of bushland were destroyed. What happened was a great tragedy. It is so true that fire is a good servant, but a bad master.

The Bible in many places speaks about fire, and almost every time it is referring to the judgement of God upon wickedness. The writer to the Hebrews tells us in frightening words: 'Our God is a consuming fire' (Hebrews 12:29).

A good example of this truth is when God destroyed those wicked cities of Sodom and Gomorrah. When righteous Lot and his family had escaped from Sodom we read, 'Then the Lord rained brimstone and fire on Sodom and Gomorrah, from the Lord out of the heavens' (Genesis 19:24).

Our God is holy and detests sin and sinners. The psalmist tells us, 'God is a just judge, and God is angry with the wicked every day' (Psalm 7:11). Because God hates sin, he will judge sin and sinners. All who have not trusted in Jesus Christ for the forgiveness of their sins will be cast into hell. As our text tells us, hell is described as 'everlasting fire'.

In Revelation 21:8 we read, 'But the cowardly, unbelieving, abominable, murderers, sexually immoral, sorcerers, idolaters, and all liars shall have their part in the lake which burns with fire and brimstone, which is the second death.'

All who are not trusting in and following the Lord Jesus Christ will be punished for their sins. As you have read in today's reading, 'And the smoke of their torment ascends for ever and ever; and they have no rest day or night, who worship the beast and his image, and whoever receives the mark of his name' (Revelation 14:11).

These are frightening words, and they are meant to be frightening, for hell is a real place. But hell holds no fears for God's people. All who are trusting in Jesus for their salvation will enter heaven, and there enjoy God's love and blessings for ever.

Reader, I pray that you are truly trusting in Christ alone for the forgiveness of your sins. May God bless you!

Activities

● ●

a. What are some of the uses of fire?
b. Name three things fire is used to describe in the Bible.

'I'm scared of the dark!'

Read
Matthew 22:1-14

'Then the king said to the servants, "Bind him hand and foot, take him away, and cast him into outer darkness; there will be weeping and gnashing of teeth"' (Matthew 22:13).

Do you know that the Lord Jesus Christ spoke more about hell than he did about heaven? He described hell in many ways. He called it 'the bottomless pit' (Revelation 9:1-2) as well as 'the lake which burns with fire and brimstone' (Revelation 21:8) .

These words give us a picture of something that is too horrible to imagine. It teaches us that sin is very evil in the sight of a holy God, and that sinners who do not repent and trust in Jesus will be punished for their sins. Jesus also described hell in the words of our text: 'outer darkness'.

Now I don't know about you, but I have a granddaughter Aimee who is afraid of the darkness. When she is put to bed each night, she says her prayers and then makes sure that the light is left turned on. Her mother and father, Lisa and Todd, have purchased a special night-light that is always on during the night.

When my own children were young, two of them, Heather and Vicki, decided they would not eat their vegetables for tea. At first my wife and I tried to encourage them by telling them how good vegetables were for growing children. But they had made up their minds that they would not eat their vegetables that night. My wife and I were upset with the girls and told them so. When they left the table they were not in a good mood at all. We could hear them in their room, talking to one another. They were making some noise and when my wife and I looked in, we saw them packing their school bags with clothes, some toys and some biscuits.

My wife and I waited in the lounge room for them to come out.

When they appeared at the door Vicki, who was about six years old, said, 'We're not happy at home and we've decided to leave and go somewhere else to live.' My wife asked them what they had in their bags and when they showed us, she suggested they would need some money and something to drink. She even said they had better take a rug with them as it would be cold outside.

At this time we were living in an isolated country schoolhouse. There were no houses near our home and certainly no street lights. We asked the two girls, 'Are you sure you want to leave home?'

'Yes,' they both replied.

Before we opened the front door for them we switched on the front light. It was quite dark outside, but the electric light made things look quite safe. We kissed the girls goodbye, opened the door and out they went with their bags over their shoulders. They turned to wave goodbye and walked down the steps. Then I closed the front door and turned off the light.

Almost at once we could hear the girls crying out in fear. We heard their footsteps as they raced up the front steps and soon they were banging on the front door.

'Let us in! Let us in, please, Mum and Dad!' they cried. We opened the door and hugged them both. That was the one and only time the two girls tried to leave home. They hated the darkness because it frightened them. It was dark, but not completely dark, for the moon and the stars were shining.

The girls are now mothers and they eat their vegetables, but I sometimes notice that their children say they don't want vegetables for tea. I hear my daughters telling their children they should eat their vegetables, because it will help them to grow up big and strong.

As an adult, the darkness of night holds no fears for me. However, some years ago, when my wife and I were on holiday we went into a deep cave. The guide turned out the lights after warning us that everything would appear black.

We could see nothing. It was so dark that the darkness seemed to touch me and I was frightened. I just could not move. I couldn't even reach out my hand to touch my wife who was near me. My wife and I, and the other people with us, were very relieved when the lights were turned on again.

In the parable Jesus told, recorded in Matthew 22:1-14, we read of a king who gave his son a wonderful wedding when he was married. Many of the people who were invited to the wedding did not come, so the king sent his servants out to ask everyone they met to come to the feast.

This parable speaks of the gospel of salvation being offered to people from all parts of the world. Jesus had come to the Jewish people, for they were God's special people. But they didn't want Christ and crucified him. The gospel was then taken to the Gentiles — all who were not Jewish.

In Christ's parable a wonderful feast was taking place. As the guests entered the king's palace they were given a special coat to wear. But the king found one person who did not have on the wedding coat. That person had not come through the doorway into the palace, but had sneaked in some other way. The king ordered his servants to take that man, bind him with ropes and throw him out into outer darkness.

In the darkness, the man would be terrified. He would be able to see the light in the king's palace; he would be able to hear the wedding guests laughing and having a good time, but he would not be able to enter.

Jesus is teaching us that if we want to go to heaven, there is only one way, and that is through faith in him. It means we do not trust in our works, our going to church, our godly parents, or anything else. It means that if we are to get to heaven we must trust in Jesus alone and be clothed in his perfect righteousness.

It would be the most terrible thing ever to find out on Judgement Day that you were lost because you did not trust in Jesus. If this were so, you would be cast into outer darkness, where there 'will be weeping and gnashing of teeth' (Matthew 22:13).

Activities

a. Why are people scared of the dark?
b. Why do you think hell is described as a place of 'outer darkness'?

'Sir, it's not fair!'

Read

Luke 12:35-48
and Matthew 25:14-30

'And that servant who knew his master's will, and did not prepare himself or do according to his will, shall be beaten with many stripes. But he who did not know, yet committed things worthy of stripes, shall be beaten with few. For everyone to whom much is given, from him much will be required; and to whom much has been committed, of him they will ask the more' (Luke 12:47-48).

Most schoolchildren don't like examinations, and I'm sure you are no different. I never looked forward to exams, and I was often not too happy about taking my report home. Too many times I was told, 'You can do better than that.'

I can remember giving my class a special spelling examination one Friday. Everyone was warned well in advance of what was to take place. I told the children to spend some time before the big day looking over their spelling lists. I even told them that errors would have to be written out as a means of learning the words that had been incorrectly spelt.

The day arrived and, after marking all the papers, I was happy to find out that most had done very well. But there were several who did poorly.

One of the children I knew was more interested in watching television than in doing any study. Another spent more time than he should have playing sport each afternoon. There was also one girl who had several errors.

When it came time to handing out the results I reminded the children that those with errors had a job to do. After their errors were written out the children had to present themselves to me when I would make sure they could spell the words correctly. 'All errors will be written out ten times. But Anne, you need only write them out five times,' I said.

Then the cry went up from the children who had to write their errors ten times: 'Sir, it's not fair!'

I simply asked, 'Why not?' Anne had been absent from school and was unaware that the spelling examination was to be held. So I explained to the children why I had made my decision. They then thought that maybe I was being fair after all.

It is good to be fair in every situation in which we find ourselves. We need to take into consideration all matters before we make our decisions, especially if our decisions will have an effect upon someone else.

God has warned us all of the seriousness of sin. Adam, our representative in the Garden of Eden, was clearly told of the punishment for disobeying the clear command of God concerning the fruit of 'the tree of the knowledge of good and evil'. Adam was told not to eat the fruit of that tree 'for in the day that you eat of it you shall surely die' (Genesis 2:17).

The apostle Paul again wrote this truth. He said, 'The wages of sin is death...' (Romans 6:23). This fact is seen every day around the world. We see cemeteries everywhere and they are always getting larger.

When the Lord spoke about death, he was not just speaking about the death of the body, but eternal death, which is hell.

The question is usually asked, 'But what about the people who have never heard of Christ and the gospel of salvation? Will they die eternally? Will they be cast into hell?'

The Bible answers this question. We are told that salvation is only possible through faith in Christ. Those who do not know Christ are lost. On the Day of Judgement, they will know in their hearts that they have not obeyed God, for their conscience will tell them they have sinned against what they knew to be right.

Our God is a just God — a very fair God. Our text tells us that if we know what God expects of us and we fail to carry out his commands, then we shall be beaten with many blows. However, the Bible tells us also that those people who did not know God's will and didn't obey will be beaten with few blows.

There will also be differing rewards handed out to God's people. Faithfulness to the commands of the Christ we love will bring rewards.

The matter that should concern you, my reader, is simply this: you know what God requires of you. You know that God requires you to trust in Jesus for your salvation. You have been given great privileges for you, no doubt, have a Bible in your home. Most of you will have the opportunity to go to Sunday school and worship, where you will be taught of God and his Son Jesus Christ. Because of all these privileges, God requires much of you. He commands you to believe in Christ and then show your love for him by being obedient to all of his commands.

Activities

● ●

a. Were you ever treated unfairly? When was that?
b. How is it that God's judgement will always be fair?

New heavens and a new earth

'Nevertheless we, according to his promise, look for new heavens and a new earth in which righteousness dwells' (2 Peter 3:13).

Read
Revelation 21:9-21

The Bible tells us that God will remould this earth into a new home for his people. This is something that all Christians look forward to, because it means that the Lord Jesus Christ, our Saviour, will have returned. It will mean an end to sin and death, so the new heavens and earth are something that is really exciting to think about.

I'm sure that you all like new things. Just recently my wife and I purchased a new car. It is a lovely white colour. It is sparkling clean and has that great 'new car' smell about it. Because it is new, it gets washed every week, not like the old car which was washed only when we had to do it.

I would like to tell you a story about a small boy who tried to help his Mum and Dad get a new car. This is a true story, even though it is hard to believe. I was teaching at a small, two-teacher school, that was cleaned by a local lady. She and her husband had bought a brand new car. They really took care of it.

One day their son and his wife and a grandson visited them. They parked their old Volkswagen in the driveway and went to have a look at the new car in the garage. The grandson heard his father say, 'Dad, you sure have a nice new car. We would like to get one, but at the moment we can't afford it. The

185

car really only needs a coat of paint and it will last for a few more years.'

Everyone then walked inside the house and, like adults usually do, they sat down and began to talk. The young boy asked his father if he could go outside and play in the yard. The adults were pleased to see young Leighton leave the lounge room. At least they wouldn't have to worry about any breakages as he touched things in Grandma's house.

Leighton looked about for something to do. He walked into the garage and looked at his grandparents' new car. Then he remembered that his father had said that all their old car needed was a coat of paint. Leighton looked about in the garage and sure enough he found a tin of paint which he quickly opened. It was still half full of paint. Soon a paint brush was in Leighton's hand.

Then he got to work. He painted his parents' car with a bright green paint. The tyres were soon done and he then set to work on the bodywork. He was happily painting the windscreen when he heard someone call, 'Leighton! Come in! Grandma has a drink for you, and there's some chocolate cake.'

Leighton was ready for something to eat. It had been hard work painting half a car. When he walked into the lounge room, his parents nearly had a fit. Their little son had green paint over most of his clothes.

'Goodness!' said his mother. 'What have you been up to?'

'I'd better go and have a look,' said his father with a very concerned look on his face.

I'm sure you can imagine everyone's surprise when they looked at a partly painted car. There were gasps of horror as the bright green paint blinded their eyes. Leighton was unconcerned: 'Look, Dad, the car's nearly new again!' he joyfully called out.

186

When Christ returns, the Bible tells us this old world which once was 'very good', but ruined by sin, will be remade. The apostle Peter tells us, 'The heavens and the earth which now exist are kept in store … reserved for fire until the day of judgement and destruction of ungodly men… But the day of the Lord will come as a thief in the night, in which the heavens will pass away with a great noise, and the elements will melt with fervent heat; both the earth and the works that are in it will be burned up' (2 Peter 3:7,10).

God will remould this world as a perfect and beautiful home for Christ and his people. Peter also tells us something about the new heavens and earth: 'Nevertheless we, according to his promise, look for new heavens and a new earth in which righteousness dwells.'

The apostle John also writes about the new creation. We read, 'There shall be no more curse, but the throne of God and of the Lamb shall be in it, and His servants shall serve Him. They shall see His face, and His name shall be on their foreheads. And there shall be no night there: They need no lamp nor light of the sun, for the Lord God gives them light. And they shall reign for ever and ever' (Revelation 22:3-5).

This new creation sounds a wonderful place in which to live. John also says of the life God's people will live in their new home: 'And God will wipe away every tear from their eyes; there shall be no more death, nor sorrow, nor crying; and there shall be no more pain, for the former things have passed away' (Revelation 21:4).

Reader, this is something that all of God's people can look forward to with real joy in their hearts. In that new and eternal kingdom, which God will make, there will be perfect happiness as we serve and worship the Lord Jesus Christ.

We shall be able to see Jesus face to face and speak with him. And we shall meet all of God's people from every age of the earth's history. Moses will be there, as will be Noah. We shall meet Samson, and we shall meet all of our godly relatives and friends who have died in faith, loving the Lord Jesus Christ.

How, then, should we live today in preparation for this wonderful day when Christ returns to take us to that new home which God has made for us? Well, we know that we must have faith in Christ for our salvation, but the apostle Peter says something more to all of God's people. 'Therefore, since all these things will be dissolved, what manner of persons ought you to be in holy conduct and godliness, looking for and hastening the coming of the day of God… Therefore, beloved, looking forward to these things, be diligent to be found by Him in peace, without spot and blameless…' (2 Peter 3:11,12,14).

Reader, live your life as if Christ were to return in a moment's time. Ever be ready, for we do not know the hour or the minute when Christ will return. Just be ready to meet your Saviour.

Activities

● ●

a. List ten problems you can see in the world today.
b. Are people behaving better today than they were hundreds of years ago?
c. What will make heaven a really wonderful place?

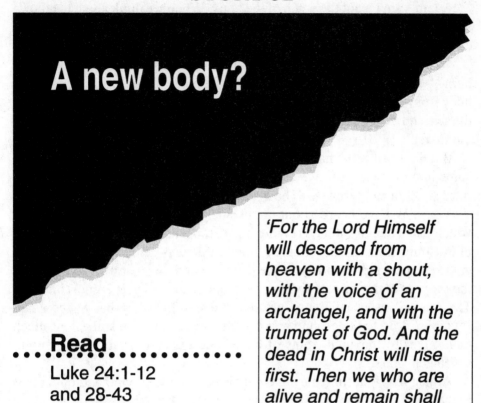

A new body?

Read
Luke 24:1-12
and 28-43

'For the Lord Himself will descend from heaven with a shout, with the voice of an archangel, and with the trumpet of God. And the dead in Christ will rise first. Then we who are alive and remain shall be caught up together with them in the clouds to meet the Lord in the air. And thus we shall always be with the Lord' (1 Thessalonians 4:16-17).

When I look into the mirror each morning I notice that I am changing. My hair is getting thinner, and what is left is getting grey. I notice that my trousers are tighter than they were before and I have more aches and pains than when I was young.

I put on my glasses, then take out my teeth and clean them. I suppose one of these days I will be able to put a hearing aid in my ear. The truth is, I am not as I used to be. My body is wearing out! I still feel good on the inside, but I can't do the things I used to do.

One day, unless the Lord Jesus comes beforehand, I will die and be buried in the ground. My body will return to the dust just as God told Adam when he sinned, 'For dust you are, and to dust you shall return' (Genesis 3:19).

Adam's sin meant the death of the body. When we think about death, we should realize how terrible sin is. Our bodies grow old and die. Sometimes even young babies die. We all die because of sin.

When Christ returns, the resurrection of every human who has ever been born — both good and wicked — will take place. Christ will gather every body from the soil (the cemetery will be a very busy place on that day!), from the sea, and even from space itself, if spacemen die and their bodies are left out there.

But the Lord Jesus has done a wonderful work for all of his people. He came into the world to save us. Part of that great salvation is that when he returns, all of his people will be given a new and glorious body.

You may have heard about the cicada. They are very unusual insects which make a high-pitched ringing noise, especially at night. In some parts of Australia the noise they make in their millions is so loud that people can't get to sleep at night. And the noise just keeps going on and on. We are told they are one of the longest-living insects and their life cycle is most unusual. The mother insect lays eggs on tree twigs. When they hatch, the small 'nymphs' drop to the ground and dig themselves into the soil. They attach themselves to the small roots of a tree and there some remain for up to seventeen years.

At just the right time they leave their hole in the ground and out comes a cicada in a shell. The cicada crawls up a tree trunk where its shell splits open and out comes, not a 'nymph', but an adult cicada, to sing for all its worth, and drive people mad with its loud noise, especially when there might be several million living in the trees beside houses.

It is strange, but only the male cicada makes a noise. The female is dumb. Some of the ancient Greeks knew this, and used to say:

Happy are the cicadas' lives,
For they have voiceless wives.

What comes out of the ground is so different to the 'nymph' or grub that goes into the ground. The mature cicada can fly about and call out.

The cicada reminds me of what is promised in the Scriptures to all those who die before the return of Christ. Our text concerns the Christians at Thessalonica who knew that Jesus would one day return. But some of their Christian friends and relatives had died and they asked the apostle Paul what would happen to these dear Christian people. Paul told them that even though the bodies of their dead were placed in the ground, their souls were with Christ in heaven.

Paul went on to say that Christ would bring with him the souls of all

Christians who had died and the souls would be reunited with their bodies: 'Behold I tell you a mystery: We shall not all sleep [die], but we shall all be changed — in a moment, in the twinkling of an eye, at the last trumpet. For the trumpet will sound, and the dead will be raised incorruptible, and we shall be changed. For this corruptible must put on incorruption, and this mortal must put on immortality. So when this corruptible has put on incorruption, and this mortal has put on immortality, then shall be brought to pass the saying that is written: "Death is swallowed up in victory." "O Death, where is your sting? O Hades, where is your victory?"' (1 Corinthians 15:51-55).

On the day of our resurrection we shall have new bodies — bodies like that of the Lord Jesus Christ. They will be glorious bodies. I'm sure I'll have a head of hair again, and won't need my glasses or false teeth. Our wrinkles, caused by ageing, will be gone.

We can't really imagine how wonderful our new bodies will be, but the Bible tells us, 'Beloved, now we are children of God; and it has not yet been revealed what we shall be, but we know that when He is revealed, we shall be like Him [Christ], for we shall see Him as He is' (1 John 3:2). And the apostle Paul wrote, 'Eye has not seen, nor ear heard, nor have entered into the heart of man the things which God has prepared for those who love Him' (1 Corinthians 2:9).

We have no real idea of what we shall be like when the resurrection takes place. For a moment, think of a small seed which has fallen to the ground. Soon it is covered and there in the ground the seed begins to think, 'I wonder what I will be like when I grow and come out of the ground? I suppose I'll be a great big seed.'

Then when the seed appears, it grows into a huge green tree in which the birds can perch. The little seed had no idea of what lay before it.

But this we know, that when Jesus returns we shall be like him — perfect in holiness, having a body like his glorious body, a body that will never age and never die.

Reader, if you are a Christian, you will one day meet all those who have died loving Christ and spend eternity with them, serving, worshipping and praising God. We shall ever be with Jesus in the new creation. It is a true saying: 'The best is yet to come!'

And what about those who are not Christians? In the book of Daniel we read of the resurrection of the godless. They will rise 'to shame and everlasting contempt' (Daniel 12:2).

Reader, just trust in Jesus and all will be well with you on the day when Christ returns. May God bless you!

Activities

●●●

a. What are some of the problems with your body?
b. If you could make five changes with yourself, what changes would you want to make?
c. What do you think will be the most wonderful thing about the new body God will give to you when Christ returns?

If these readings have been a spiritual blessing to you please send a postcard of your homeland to:

James A. Cromarty,
3 Appaloosa Place,
Wingham. N.S.W.
Australia 2429.